Copyright, Legal Notice and Disclaimer:

Copyright 2011 By Gavin Holmes. All rights reserved.

This publication is protected under the US Copyright Act of 1976 and all other applicable international, federal, state and local laws, and all rights are reserved, including resale rights.

No part of this publication may be reproduced, stored in a retrieval system, or transmitted in any form or by any means, electronic, mechanical, photocopying, recording, scanning or otherwise, except as permitted under section 107 or 108 of the US Copyright Act of 1976, without either the prior written permission of the publisher.
All charts herein are provided with the permission of TradeGuider Systems International (www.tradeguider.com)

Limit of Liability and Disclaimer of Warranty: The publisher has used its best efforts in preparing this book, and the information provided herein is provided for educational purposes only. The publisher makes no representation or warranties with respect to the accuracy or completeness of the contents of this book and specifically disclaims any implied warranties of merchantability or fitness for any particular purpose and shall in no event be liable for any loss of profit or any other commercial damage, including but not limited to special, incidental, consequential, or other damages.

Trading Stocks, Commodities, Futures, Options on Futures, and retail off-exchange foreign currency transactions involves substantial risk of loss and is not suitable for all investors. You should carefully consider whether trading is suitable for you in light of your circumstances, knowledge, and financial resources. You may lose all or more of your initial investment. Opinions, market data, and recommendations are subject to change at any time.

ISBN: 978-0-9836268-0-0

Trading
in the Shadow
of the Smart Money

The Secret of Market Manipulation Revealed

Understand How to Read Charts Like
Smart Money Professionals and
Become Profitable by Using Volume Spread Analysis™

By Gavin Holmes

TABLE OF CONTENTS

ACKNOWLEDGEMENTS

FOREWARD

INTRODUCTION
The VSA Methodology: Background to Volume Spread Analysis
The Players

CHAPTER 1
The Meeting that Changed My Life

CHAPTER 2
The Game on Wall Street: Market Manipulation

CHAPTER 3
The Smart Money and the Not-So-Smart Money

CHAPTER 4
Beware of The News!

CHAPTER 5
How to Read Charts like a Professional Trader

CHAPTER 6
Key Principles of the VSA Methodology
Part 1: Weakness

CHAPTER 7
Key Principles of the VSA Methodology
Part 2: Strength

CHAPTER 8
Developing a Personal Trading Plan Using Volume Spread Analysis

CHAPTER 9
The Power of Belief in Your Trading System

CHAPTER 10
Reasons Why Retail Traders and Investors Lose Money

CHAPTER 11
Interviews with International Wyckoff and Volume Spread Analysis Experts

CHAPTER 12
Advice from the Master, Tom Williams

ACKNOWLEDGEMENTS

So many people have helped me write this book. In the process, they have also helped me find my purpose in life! The names would fill over ten pages, but to keep this brief, allow me to acknowledge and thank the following people:

Firstly, my heart goes out to everyone who pushed me into completing my book. The project took over two years to finish, but it was a very worthwhile adventure, indeed.

Broadly, I would like to thank all of our TradeGuider customers and VSA club members for their continued support an encouragement as we have reached our tenth anniversary n business!

I want to especially thank and acknowledge hard work of TradeGuider customer, Eric Rivera, for helping us program the scanner add-in for TradeGuider version 3 which launched in 2008. My sincere gratitude is also extended to TradeGuider customers, William Donelson and Malcolm Moos, who made excellent suggestions incorporated into this book.

I must acknowledge VSA expert and fund manager, Philip Friston, for all his tireless work in helping Tom Williams write the new VSA dialogue boxes for the TradeGuider software, as well as his dedicated contribution to the VSA club.

Thanks to VSA expert Sebastian Manby, Wyckoff experts Dr. Gary Dayton and David Weis, for contributing their interviews to this book. I appreciate the time and effort to help give your expert opinions to assist the traders and investors who read my book.

I would like to acknowledge the great traders and educators I have met who have worked with me on various projects. I have learned a great deal through collaborating with Markus Heitkoetter, Todd Krueger, Roy Didlock, Rob Hoffman, Gary Fullet, Philip Friston, Dr. Gary Dayton, David Weiss, Professor Hank Pruden, Bruce Frazier, Harvey Loomstein, Adrienne Toghraie, Brad Bedford-Brown, Bill Wermine, Martin Wong, and Nick Radge.

Paul Avins, thank you for inspiring me in the early days to take massive action! You motivated me to improve my life, as well as the life of others!

Richard Seegers, a dedicated TradeGuider customer was kind enough to take the time and patience to help add insight to the list of topics and content of the book. Thank you, Richard, for your input and expertise.

I give a very special thanks to Jim Mooney and Jim Cagnina from Infinity Futures in Chicago. Hey have consistently supported TradeGuider, and even myself, personally. As a result, we have become great friends! I must also acknowledge all the brokers at Infinity for their support, including Jeff Kaprelian and Andy Delap. They are real first class guys to deal with and are always there when you need them.

Mike Panice, my broker at PFG Best helped me get permission to re-print the interview with Tim Rayment. Thank you, Mike, for your assistance and support.

I cannot forget the entire TradeGuider Team! These people are the backbone of the company and continually support the business for me and my partner, Richard Bednall. These people are Chief Technical Officer AJ Robinson, my brother Darren Holmes, Peter and Rita Offen (who are always there to help Tom), our new business development team Josh Davidson and Michael Margolese, our programmer Robert Harwood, and all of our VSA club contributors. A very special thank you goes to our head of public relations and marketing for TradeGuider Systems International, Armi Matienzo, who has worked extremely hard on completing production for this book on all aspects. Well done, Armi.

Dallas Badham is also very much part of the TradeGuider Team and I would like to thank her for always taking great care of me as she does Tom when I visit him in Worthing, England. Thank you, Dallas, for your hospitality.

Special thanks to my father-in-law, Kent Woodham, for keeping the finances in order, which is obviously critical in any business!

A great big thank you goes out to my business partner and friend, Richard Bednall, who takes my hair brained ideas and makes them happen! Without Richard, there would be no websites or emails to reach out to people to get our message out there day after day.

A son's thank you to my loving mum, Shirley. Thank you for being such a wonderful mother! I must also thank my brother Darren for his unflinching support.

I want to thank two very special people from the bottom of my heart who have made a serious impact on my life. Firstly, Tom Williams, the man who inspired many thousands of traders and investors worldwide to better understand the importance of supply and demand and the significance of chart reading. He passed on that knowledge unselfishly and graciously, and is viewed as a true hero to many. We owe a great deal to the likes of Tom, especially Richard Ney and Richard Wyckoff. These men all had the same goal to share the wisdom and help others.

Last and definitely not least, an extraordinary thank you goes to my very patient and understanding wife, Laura. She pushed me to get to the office and write the book as the deadline grew closer. If it weren't for her, I'd still be writing the introduction! Thank you Laura, I love you very much, as well as my darling children, Nathan, Olivia, and Ryan. They are all little characters in their own way, but they are a real blessing that completes me.

FOREWORD

When I first met Gavin over ten years ago, I explained to him how the financial markets operated. I remember his reaction of surprise and bewilderment. Gavin knew very little about trading and investing, but he clearly had an appetite to learn and was hungry for success. It was for this reason I knew he had potential to become a great trader.

When I wrote my first book, *"The Undeclared Secrets that Drive the Stock Market"*, I had no idea how popular it would become, but as time passed, I knew I needed to pass on my extensive knowledge to someone who had the same passion to help and teach others as I do. Gavin fit the bill perfectly. Despite having setbacks, h has always maintained a very positive attitude to life and a willingness to let me teach him everything I know about trading.

During one of his many times staying with me in Worthing, England, I explained to Gavin that writing my book was one of the most rewarding and satisfying things I have accomplished. I suggested that he seriously think about following in my footsteps and write a book. He has clearly learned a great deal since I first met him, but I really didn't think he was going to sit down and actually write a book, as he is a bit of a live wire, so to see a 200 page book appear in 2011 was wonderful!

I had *"Trading in the Shadow of the Smart Money"* read to me (I am now 84 with limited vision and suffer from macular degeneration) and I was pleasantly surprised at just how good this book is. HE has explained in a clear and easy to understand manner the ways of how you can make money in the financial markets if you comprehend the underlying mechanics implement a system and a plan.

I certainly recommend this book and keep it as a reference at all times. It gives great insight into how a trader enters the market as a winner. Gavin has become an excellent trader in his own right.

It appears to me that potential traders who enter the market with absolutely no previous experience seem to do very well, much more so than traders who have continually jumped from one system to the next, spending much time and money in search of the elusive 'Holy Grail' of trading. The ones that waste their efforts in search for the perfect trading machine end up with no system and no plan. As a result, they will fail. If there is a Holy Grail for traders, the closest thing is the information contained within this book!

If a trader enters the market with an unpolluted mind, they will clearly see that the VSA principles are present in all markets, in all time frames, and will recognize how they all work in order to identify profitable trade set-ups. Those traders will then develop and grow their trading skills around this knowledge.

Most traders and investors do not understand Volume implications and how important it is in their analysis of any of the markets in any time frame. Basically, you have hundreds of thousands of traders constantly trading: some go long, some short, others are holding or waiting to get into the market, while others may already be in profitable positions or perhaps in losing positions.

So how on earth can we possibly make sense of this? It is not difficult as you might think. Whenever a trade is entered in, the appropriate exchange registers this as Volume on a continuous basis. So to us, **Volume represents activity**.

Now, what is the exact amount of activity taking place in relation to the price bar on your chart? The activity must be the reason why the chart is behaving the way it is. You then need to realize that at least 80% (or even more) of that Volume will be the professional money, or the Smart Money, as Gavin refers to it in his book. In other words, they are the traders who are trading large amounts of money and contracts that are large enough to alter the direction of the market.

On your chart, for example, if you see an up bar that has moved into fresh high ground with a narrow Spread and the Volume is very high, the TradeGuider software I invented will automatically produce a *Sign of Weakness* indicator. This reason for this is that the professional money has to sell as the market goes up. The narrow Spread up bar is caused by them satisfying every buy order that comes into the market, in other words, capping the top end of the market, or like putting a lid on it.

This produces a narrow Spread on the up-bar and Gavin shows several excellent examples of this price action in his book. If the activity is very high, then this can only tell you that professional money is taking their profits and the net effect of this is to make the market bearish (in other words, weak).

Very often it will be difficult for you to see this because the news will inevitably be good and it is hard for people to understand that you need to sell on good news. By their very nature, most traders will consider themselves to be quite intelligent and maybe have previous success in life that will show this.

So you have to ask yourself, "Why is it so difficult to predict market behavior?"

All the skills you acquired during your lifetime never seemed to be quite good enough, so why is this? I would say the reason for this is that all the information (and I mean all) that is pouring into your mind cannot be the correct information. It is this deluge of misinformation that is making it difficult to predict market behavior on a regular and reliable basis.

This book goes a long way to broaden and fulfill your understanding of exactly what is going on. You can only benefit from this information and this information will be with you for the rest of your life

-Tom Williams

INTRODUCTION
The VSA Methodology: Background to Volume Spread Analysis

TradeGuider is based on a methodology called *Volume Spread Analysis, or VSA.*

Following is a brief explanation of TradeGuider Systems' software and the use of its inherent presentation and processes of Volume Spread Analysis. I aim to also explain the software's role in being able to assist traders to recognize *market manipulation* in order to make consistent and successful decisions. I will show you chart examples of how professional activity is clearly visible in all markets and all time frames, especially if you know what to look for.

Volume Spread Analysis is a proprietary market analysis method conceived by Tom Williams, Chairperson of TradeGuider Systems. The VSA method works particularly well at highlighting the imbalances of supply and demand.

VSA is utilized in the TradeGuider software to analyze a market by observing the interrelationship between *Volume, Price, and the Spread* (or range) of the price bar.

TradeGuider was previously known as *Wyckoff Volume Spread Analysis* and has been in existence for over 20 years. Driven by an artificial intelligence engine, TradeGuider VSA is unique and is capable of analyzing any liquid market in any time frame by extracting the information it needs in order to indicate the imbalances of supply and demand evident in a chart. In doing so, TradeGuider is able to graphically exhibit the essential dynamics of market movement.

The software functions in Real-Time (RT) or End-Of-Day (EOD) modes. It enables users to see when the professional money, or what I refer to as **the Smart Money**, are entering, exiting, or abstaining from participating in the market being traded. This will empower clients to make intelligible and more informed trading decisions. The TradeGuider VSA method is a revolutionary concept that can be used on its own or in conjunction with other trading platforms. It makes an ideal choice for both adding value to data vendor platforms and decision support. For any liquid market, this provides the best supply and demand analysis in the business. The extensive expert system is easy to use and has an innate understanding of market dynamics and Volume.

The sophisticated expert system is augmented by a novel set of proprietary tools that confirm trade set-ups as they appear in any time frame and in any market. The indicators are displayed automatically on the chart and there is no configuration, no setting of parameters, and no optimization. Our belief is that if a system requires optimization, to make it work, then the basis of that particular methodology cannot have been sound in the first place. The process of optimization is used to cover up a whole range of flaws in the original analysis method(s). Instead, our concepts are robust and can be applied to any time frame with consistent results.

As mentioned earlier, this is not a new concept. Tom Williams, the inventor of VSA is a former syndicate trader. He observed the markets were being manipulated and that the key to unlocking the truth lay in the relationship between the *Volume, the Spread of the bar, and the Closing Price*. Tom spent many years studying the concepts of Richard Wyckoff, a renowned trader of the 1920's and 1930's.

Wyckoff wrote several books about trading the markets and he eventually created the Stock Market Institute in Phoenix, Arizona. At its core, Wyckoff's work is based on the analysis of trading ranges and determining when the stocks are in basing markdown, distribution, or mark-up phases. Incorporated into these phases are ongoing shifts between weak hands, or public ownership, which again, is now commonly known as the Smart Money.

When Tom Williams went back to Beverly Hills in the early 1980's, he began to investigate the possibility of computerizing the system he had learned as a syndicate trader – and so began the evolution of Volume Spread Analysis. With the assistance of an experienced computer programmer, Tom carefully studied thousands of charts to recognize the obvious patterns that were left when the Smart Money were active. This technique, although simple in concept, took several years to write and is now taught as a methodology in combination with software known as TradeGuider.

Volume Spread Analysis seeks to establish the cause of price movements. The cause, quite simply, is the imbalance between supply and demand, or strength and weakness, in a liquid market. This is created by the activity of the Smart Money. If you use the TradeGuider software, you will notice that it does an excellent job of detecting these key imbalances for you, thereby taking the hard work out of reading the markets an enabling you to fully concentrate on your trading.

To use a chart without Volume is like buying a car without a gas tank. The significance and importance of Volume seems to be little understood by most non-professional traders. Perhaps this is due to the fact there is sparse information and very limited instruction available on this vital aspect of technical analysis.

For the correct analysis of Volume, one needs to realize the recorded Volume information contains only half of the knowledge required for a correct analysis. The other half of the meaning is found in the price Spread. Volume indicates the amount of activity going on and the corresponding price Spread shows the price movement on that Volume. Most traders can't believe you can't analyze Volume in the forex markets because that information is unavailable. That is simply not true. Later in this book I will show you how TradeGuider proprietary system does something those traders thought impossible.

Some technical indicators attempt to combine both Volume and price movements together, but this approach has its limitations. At times, the market will go up on high Volume, but also know it can go up on low Volume! The obvious conclusion is that there are other factors in paly.

Price and Volume are intimately linked and their interrelationship is a complex one, which is the main reason why TradeGuider was developed. As mentioned previously, the system is capable of analyzing the markets in real-time (RT) or at the end of the day (EOD), displaying any one of the 400 indicators on the screen to show the imbalances of supply and demand (for more information, please visit www.tradeguider.com).

THE PLAYERS

Now let's briefly look at the inspiration for this book and the teachers that had an impact in their time in helping others to understand 'the game'.

Richard Demille Wyckoff (November 2, 1873 – March 19, 1934) was a stock market authority, founder and one-time editor of the *"Magazine of Wall Street"* (founded in 1907) and editor of *"Stock Market Technique"*. He worked in New York City during a 'golden age' for technical analysis that existed during the early decades of the 20th Century. Wyckoff became wealthy through trading in the stock market, but he also became altruistic about the public's Wall Street experience (visit www.richardwyckoff.org for more information).

"Thousands of those who operate in the markets now recognize the fact that the market momentarily indicates its own immediate future, and that these indications are accurately recorded in the market transactions second by second, and therefore those who can interpret what transactions take place second by second or moment by moment have a distinct advantage over the general trading public..."

"Tape reading seems to us, the science of determining from the tape the immediate trend of prices."

"It is a method of forecasting from what appears on the tape now, what is likely to appear in the future."

Richard D. Wyckoff
Studies in Tape Reading
Rollo Tape

Richard Ney (November 12, 1915-July 18, 2004) was an actor, financier, creator of The Ney Report, and author of best-selling investment books such as The Wall Street Jungle. He is considered to be the "Father of the Specialist Theory", and was an extremely successful investor, money manager, investment advisor, and self-made millionaire. He was also the foremost authority on the manipulation of stock prices by Specialists and insiders on the floor of the New York Stock Exchange.

Richard Ney's Rolls Royce- the number plate it says it all (Wake Up)!

 **Tom Williams is the inventor of the TradeGuider System methodology called Volume Spread Analysis, also known as VSA. Tom was introduced to day trading while working in Beverly Hills for a boss of an elite group of trading syndicates. Through them, he learned the secrets of how the markets really worked and eventually became a successful syndicate trader in his own right. Now in his eighties, Tom has written two books and still trades to this day (early 2011).**

"The market is devious and many times you will buy on good news only to lose money and sell on bad news only to see the price rise soon afterwards, and that is because the Smart Money understand crowd behavior and take full advantage of the 'Herd'!!

"The market works because human beings have two powerful emotions that they have difficulty controlling, namely fear and greed."

"The market has to be fed losers. It is devious and what you hear will often not be the truth. I have never heard the truth about the stock market or any market on television. Just look at the news about the oil market in May 2008. Greed at the top, as many traders piled in because they were told oil had to go to $200 a barrel! The chart never lies and Gavin went on YouTube to show the TradeGuider proprietary signal, namely 'The End of a Rising Market'. Then look at the banking sector in 2008 during September. Fear set in and professional money began to buy not sell and that caused stocks like Goldman Sachs to Rally 400%. It was all in the chart if you know how to analyze supply and demand".

Tom Williams
Master the Markets

CHAPTER 1
The Meeting That Changed My Life

I remember the phone call well. It was an early Monday morning and my personal assistant, Anne, came into my office to tell me there was a gentleman from Yorkshire, England on the phone. He had seen one of my e-marketing websites and had a proposition for me. I asked Anne to get more information from him before she put the call through. Apparently, this gentleman named Roy Didlock was involved with the development of a computerized trading program called Wyckoff Volume Spread Analysis. The inventor of the program, Tom Williams, a retired syndicate trader, wanted to partner with a marketing firm in order to bring his trading software to a wider audience.

I knew absolutely nothing about trading and investing at the time, but I was curious, so I took the call. Roy, on the other end of the line, had a deep and pleasant voice with a thick Yorkshire accent. He began to explain how Tom had started the company as a hobby (to me, this implied that they had no marketing budget). The company Tom had founded several years prior, Genie Software Ltd., was interested in partnering with a marketing or advertising agency, and in return, the marketing arm would take a share for its services.

At the outset I was skeptical, but somewhat intrigued, especially by Roy's approach. Roy told me he picked about 60 companies he found off the internet and we were one of the companies that had suitable qualifications to fit their purposes. When I asked him how many phone calls and visits he had made and what type of response he had received, in a dejected tone he simply said we were one of the last companies on his list. I could sense that it was an issue to work without a marketing budget and it most likely that there had been little or no interest in the software.

At this point, a little voice in my head urged me to invite him to the office to find out more. In those days, my office was in Beckenham, Kent, which is about 400 miles (530 kilometers) from Yorkshire. I asked Roy if he could provide me with a business plan and whether it would be possible for him to come down from his base upcountry to visit me at my office in the south so we could discuss this proposal. I was a bit surprised by his enthusiasm. He jumped at my suggestion and we set a meeting up immediately for the following week and Roy informed me that Tom Williams would also come along so he could explain how the financial markets really work. I was fascinated, to say the least, and it seemed as if time moved slower as I as I eagerly anticipated the meeting.

Roy and Tom arrived early and were asked to wait in the boardroom. The day was already hectic with my extremely busy exhibition design company and e-marketing business. I felt that I could give Roy and Tom 45 minutes out of my chaotic day to see their business plan. That should be enough time, I thought- meet with them briefly now, take it away, and digest its contents later.

There were two very well dressed men waiting for me in the boardroom. Roy greeted me first and eagerly shook my hand. He told me he used to work for Ernst and Young Cap Gemini, one of the world's largest management consulting, outsourcing, and professional services companies. Roy then quickly turned to introduce Tom Williams. He was an elderly gentleman. I estimated him to be in his early seventies, but was impressed at how highly alert and articulate he was.

This was going to be an interesting meeting.

Roy handed me their business plan, which was well prepared and very organized, and started his presentation. As I mentioned before, I knew almost nothing about the financial markets at that time. Unfortunately, after about fifteen minutes into his presentation I still ceased to have the faintest idea what he was talking about. I wanted to call the meeting to an end and get on with the rest of my busy day. Tom, on the other hand, was not going to let that happen! He already noticed my impatient body language during the presentation.

Just as I was about to speak, Tom, being the distinguished gentleman that he is, raised his hand in the air and said, "Stop, Roy." With a glint in his eye and hand still in the air he then said, "Gavin, let's go back to the beginning and let me explain to you how the markets *really* work!"

With no hesitation Tom began to explain the markets to me.

"All financial markets move on the Universal Law of Supply and Demand. When you say this to any trader or investor, they will all nod in agreement and say, 'Well that is obvious. Tell me something new!' However, what they do *not* understand is how to correctly pull this information out of a price chart. It took me several years to develop a computer program called Wyckoff Volume Spread Analysis, or Wyckoff VSA, which does exactly that. It extracts the supply and demand information on a chart to give clear signals when the big players, or what I call **the Smart Money**, are very active or inactive in order for the user to trade in harmony with the Smart Money moves."

Tom continued, "You know Gavin, the markets do not move by accident! They are not as random as many traders and investors think. They are, however, deliberately manipulated to wrong-foot the unsuspecting and uninformed traders, which I call **the Herd**. If you can read supply and demand by analyzing Volume, you have a distinct trading advantage over the Herd in order to position yourself to trade in harmony with Smart Money!"

I gasped, "The markets are manipulated?! Come on Tom, We have regulatory bodies here in England to prevent all that." I said naively, "I have friends in the city who trade and they would laugh if you told them that!"

Tom looked at me intensely and said, "If you do not believe me, let me show you on the charts. Your eyes will be opened to the many opportunities if you can interpret the action of the manipulators."

I was spell bound. This fellow clearly knew something that I did not so I let him continue.

"How do you know all this?" I asked. There was a reason why Tom was able to retire at forty a very wealthy man, as I was to find out later.

"Well Gavin," Tom began, "in the late 1950's, I decided I wanted to make money- serious money. I was in my late twenties then and I had just sold my popular coffee house, The Whisky Go-Go in Brighton. I was also qualified as a Registered Nurse, so I figured I would make my way to Beverly Hills, California because I knew that was where the big money was- and that is exactly what I did."

Tom continued, "When I arrived in the United States, I was fortunate enough to file quickly as a Registered Nurse and joined an agency in Beverly Hills. One of my earliest assignments with this agency was working for the family of a very wealthy oil tycoon and trading syndicate member. The family was deeply worried about this individual (who I will refer to as 'George') due to his serious drug addiction that needed to be controlled. The family believed that a full-time RN was necessary to monitor his behavior. I was interviewed for this position and was chosen shortly afterwards."

"George was the boss of an elite group of trading syndicates in the United States. During that time, they traded mostly their own money, but traded some money for others in the stock market. They were very successful, but they shunned publicity. That was their nature, which is probably why very few knew of their existence."

"Their basic strategy was to target company stocks and remove what they called the *floating supply* of that stock if any of it was available on the open market. This process could take months, sometimes even years, but eventually, the syndicate would be in majority control of that particular company's stock. This phase of buying is known as **accumulation**."

"When the general market conditions appear favorable, the syndicate can then mark up the price of the stock, which is surprisingly easy since they have removed all of the floating supply and resistance to higher prices. This means that the sellers of the stock have all but disappeared. After that, there is very little stock available that can be sold once their price rally commences."

"At some time in the future, a point will be reached when the syndicate will take advantage of the higher prices obtained in the rally to take profits. They start this by selling the stock back to the uninformed traders and investors, or the Herd. This is called the **distribution phase**. It is at this point a handsome profit can be made for the syndicate and its members."

I asked Tom how the syndicate would get the Herd to buy stock at much higher prices than what the syndicate originally paid. Tom just gave a big smile as he remembered the moment he was about to share.

"I can actually remember, very clearly actually, a particular US stock which I believe is still around today. At that time, they were called Teledyne Technologies (TDY). Our syndicate had heavily accumulated them and it was time to take profits. To acquire this, any tricks are fair game. For example we would target the annual general meetings and ask bullish questions that would often be reported to the media the next day. We would 'create' as much positive news as possible in order to get the crowd excited. True or not, it was irrelevant to us, as long as people were buying the now high-priced stock from the syndicate."

"This was a very profitable business and it is one of the reasons why there are bull moves and bear moves in the markets. It is supply and demand working in the longer term. Ironically, the directors of most companies barely have an idea of why their stocks move up or down. Most will often shrug their shoulders if asked why their stock had just fallen 10%. They will have no clue why their stock declined, especially when the company is in better shape now than the previous year. To them, there appears to be no logical reason why these moves happen. However, the syndicates know better since they were actively involved in trading these stocks up and down!"

The more Tom explained the mechanics of how the financial markets operated, the more absorbed I became. The forty-five minute meeting turned into an hour and forty-five minutes! Before long, lunchtime was upon us and I instructed my personal assistant to cancel all my afternoon meetings. I had a feeling this could potentially become something very big. I decided this would be an opportunity not to be missed. As I think back now while I write about this important event 10 years later, I am happy about how right I was!

The TradeGuider journey had begun. Little did I know it back then, but Tom was grooming me to be his protégé. He would teach me everything he knew and I would learn how to read the charts just like he did.

Tom went to Beverly Hills to find his fortune. He met George, gained his trust and confidence, and became an established member of a trading syndicate that played 'the game' only insiders truly understood. It wasn't long before Tom was asked to start hand drawing the charts the syndicates would use to make their speculative attacks. On his own admission, Tom's hand-drawn charts were a work of art- it turns out that he was a natural when it came to drawing and detail.

The more Tom got involved with charting the various hand-picked stocks by the syndicate, the more inquisitive he became about what was going on with the price movement, the Volume, and where the price closed. Tom constantly asked the traders in the syndicate for information, but they were far too busy making money. So finally, they decided to send Tom to the Wyckoff Chart Reading Course in Park Ridge, Illinois just outside of Chicago. It was here that he finally got a grip on what was happening. Tom realized that all clues were in the charts if you knew how to read them correctly.

He spent twelve happy and prosperous years with the syndicate in Beverly Hills. He traveled all over the US networking and meeting many interesting people. By the age of forty, Tom had made enough money to live the rest of his life very comfortably and decided it was time to move back to England. A few years later, he purchased a facility for retired folk so he could continue his nursing and fulfill his passion for helping others.

Tom continued to trade as well, but became consumed with all the knowledge he had learned from the syndicate and its traders back in the United States. It was also at this time computers were becoming more readily available to the general public. With these thoughts in mind, Tom conjured up a brilliant idea, which he has spent the rest of his life developing and improving- he would computerize the Wyckoff Method and the knowledge he had gained from that study to produce automated trading signals that did not have to rely on human intervention. He would need a programmer skilled enough to interpret his specific instructions, so he scoured locally in Torquay, Devon, UK.

The computer would need to identify buy and sell set-ups using **Volume Spread Analysis**. This method of analyzing the market does not use past price formulas, which never seem to work. Tom was only interested in:

- **The Volume** or activity.

- **The Spread** or range of the price bar.

- **The Closing Price** or the point where the price closes on the current bar. It is the point where the bar closes that is the most important of the 3 key analysis factors. Price closes either at the bottom, the middle, or the top of the current bar. This is considered extremely significant to the analysis.

By good fortune, Tom stumbled across a newspaper advertisement for programming services situated close to where he lived. He immediately arranged a meeting, but was still unsure about whether his ideas were able to be programmed, let alone work properly to give accurate trade set-ups the methodology produced. The programmer, Robert Harwood, agreed they would at least give it a try to see what would happen.

Within weeks, the first ten indicators were programmed in and to their utter amazement, it worked! The indicators gave clear and accurate signals of supply and demand as they appeared and as the weeks went on, the indicators grew in number and were refined many times over.

As the software progressed to the point of being a usable program, a rumor radiated amongst Tom's trading friends about his new program and its astonishing accuracy. He began to sell the software for a small fee to his close friends and colleagues in the business. From these early seeds came the first version of Wyckoff Volume Spread Analysis version 1 from Genie Software Ltd (and the latest incarnation aptly named TradeGuider Real-Time (RT) and End-of-Day (EOD) software program).

Tom Williams' work was clearly groundbreaking and had enhanced the excellent work of early 1900's trader Richard Demille Wyckoff. Amongst other things, this man recognized that tape reading was the key to becoming a successful and profitable trader.

Tom left the meeting in a somber note. He looked at me and said, "Gavin, always remember that the market has to have more losers than winners. It is devious. I have never heard the truth about the market through the media."

A significant and memorable example of this is the 9/11 attacks on the World Trade Centers. If you recall, the markets closed for an entire week. During that week, the news was horrific, especially the news about the future performance of the financial markets. Once the markets opened, they did indeed plummet and many media sources were predicting an inevitable bear market. Grim-faced reporters looked at you from television screens telling you that billions of dollars were being wiped off the markets and that a collapse was inevitable.

On the surface, this news may have been partly true, but the general public will never be told the whole truth. It is highly likely that self-regulated exchanges were only too aware that all their traders were frantically buying from the panicking sellers because a bargain was to be had. A more truthful media report should have said something like this:

Good evening ladies and gentlemen. As you know, the markets have re-opened today and prices have fallen rapidly as President Bush and Prime Minister Blair have warned of further attacks. This is having a negative impact on stock prices even though these companies are still in the same shape September 12th as they were on September 10th. This panic selling seems somewhat irrational.

The good news, however, is that we have direct contact with the insiders and market specialists on the various exchange floors. They have told us that their traders are busy buying everything that is being sold by the panic-stricken Herd. You will see in a week or two that this market is not bearish at all, but in fact bullish, and the market will rise rapidly. This is due to stocks and other instruments being passed from weak holders to strong holders.

This will be clear from the massive Volume on the downside. Note that the bar has closed in the middle and not in the low. This indicates buying must be taking place, and therefore, contrary to what the news is implying, prices will go up and not down.

After this example, Tom said, "Gavin, this is an ongoing process in varying degrees of intensity. Remember, the chart never lies if you learn how to read it correctly and that is exactly what I will teach you."

After that day, I contacted my business partner, Richard Bednall, and told him of this great opportunity. After some due diligence and after speaking with some of the city traders I knew, we were convinced that this was a most worthwhile venture that would help retail traders and investors start leveling the playing field and give them an opportunity to make money in harmony with the manipulators.

My life changed after Tom taught me everything he knew. I began to see things I had never seen before. I began to read the charts as a musician would read sheet music. I felt enlightened and open minded, seeing things for what they really were and not how they were reported in the mainstream media. I promised Tom I would help him continue his work to show unenlightened traders how to find the truth, thereby becoming profitable in the markets.

So with that said, I hope you enjoy this book. I also hope you read it more than once so you can truly embrace the knowledge imparted within.

CHAPTER 2
The Game on Wall Street

Something very strange happened in the financial markets on May 6th, 2010. This day is now referred to as the **Flash Crash**. Even as I write about it more than 12 months after that eventful day, no credible explanation has been provided by the regulatory authorities as to exactly what caused the crash or who was responsible. In fact, many investors began to suspect that all was not what it seemed.

CBNC's *Closing Bell* anchor Maria Bartiromo was reporting on the day the Flash Crash happened. Below is a transcript of fellow reporter Matt Nesto explaining to Bartiromo some unusual anomalies in a number of stocks, even though the mainstream media claimed that it was caused by a lone trader from a major banking institution hitting the wrong button. 'B' for billion was entered instead of an 'M' for million while trading the CME E-mini S&P Futures! The conversation went as follows (this is also available to view on Youtube.com found using keywords, 'Maria Bartiromo, Market Manipulation'):

NESTO: A person familiar with the Citi investigation said one focus of the trading probes were the futures contracts tied to the S&P 500 stock index known as the E-mini S&P 500 futures, and in particular, that two-minute window in which 16 billion of the futures were sold... Again, those sources are telling us that Citigroup's total E-mini Volume for the entire day was only 9 billion, suggesting that the origin of the trades was elsewhere.

Nesto named eight stocks that were hit with the supposed computer error/bad trade that went all the way down to zero or one cent. These stocks include Exelon (NYSE:EXC), Accenture (NYSE:ACN), CenterPoint Energy (NYSE:CNP), Eagle Material (NYSE:EXP), Genpact Ltd (NYSE:G), ITC Holdings (NYSE:ITC), Brown & Brown (NYSE:BRO), Casey's General (NASDAQ:CASY) and Boston Beer (NYSE:SAM).

NESTO: Now according to someone else close to Citigroup's own probe of the situation, the E-Minis trade on the CME. Now Maria, I want to add something else, just in terms of these erroneous trades that Duncan Niederauer; the NYSE CEO was just talking about. I mean, we've talked a lot about Accenture. This is a Dublin-based company. It is not in any of the indexes. If you look in the S&P 500, for example, I show at least two stocks that traded to zero or one cent – Exelon and CenterPoint. If you look in the Russell 1000, I show Eagle Materials, Genpact, ITC and Brown & Brown, also trading to zero or a penny, and also Casey's General Stores, as well as Boston Beer trading today, intraday, to zero or a penny. So those have at least eight names that they're going to have to track down on top of the Accenture trade, where we have the stock price intraday showing us at least, we'll assume, a bogus trade of zero.

When Matt Nesto called these trades 'bogus', host and CNBC veteran Maria Bartiromo looked shocked and a little angry and replied:

*BARTIROMO: That is ridiculous. I mean this really sounds like **market manipulation** to me. This is outrageous.*

According to Nesto, these are frequent occurrences, at least at the NASDAQ exchange. Unfortunately, if you make a trade and lose money, there's no recourse.

NESTO: It happens a lot, Maria. It really does. I mean, we could probably ask the NASDAQ, they may not want to say how often it happens, but it happens frequently. And they go back and they correct. And the thing that stinks is if you, in good faith, put in a trade and made money and then lost it, you lose it. And there's no recourse and there's no way to appeal.

When I called Tom Williams about what happened and I mentioned that CNBC had actually reported the trading activity that day as market manipulation, Tom laughed and said jokingly, "I bet there is a signal in our TradeGuider software program showing what we call a *Shakeout*."

To my amazement, I opened the program and there it was, the proprietary TradeGuider signal *Sign of Strength 87 - Shakeout*:

SOS 87 SHAKEOUT

Note: None.

Bar Description: A *Shakeout* is a mark down on a wide Spread and closes up near the high to shake out weak holders. If Volume is low, then supply has dried up. High Volume suggests demand overcame the supply but remember this supply will hold back future upward progress. If the Spread is narrow it will have less impact.

This particular signal is more general and does not need to close near the high of the bar. Exercise caution if the bar has gapped down as this can indicate hidden weakness. If the Volume is ultra high, this can be climactic action and the start of accumulation.

Background: The background is extremely important. You should see strength in the background with *Stopping Volume* or a *Selling Climax*. Is there some minor *SOW* in an up-trend or has supply hit the market?

Future: A *Shakeout* on low Volume is really a violent test and has the same effect. It shows supply has disappeared and you would then expect higher prices.

A *Shakeout* on high Volume shows demand was prepared to absorb the supply on that bar but they will likely want to test that supply in the future. Any low Volume testing back into the area of the Shakeout would be a strong *SOS*.

Be cautious if the *Shakeout* is followed by low Volume up bars, or high Volume up bars closing in the middle, especially on a narrow Spread. If the market starts to whipsaw and goes sideways, it may be building a cause for the next up move. Remember, you need to look at the overall picture, not just the individual bars.

Copyright TradeGuider Systems, 2009

FLASH CRASH CHART

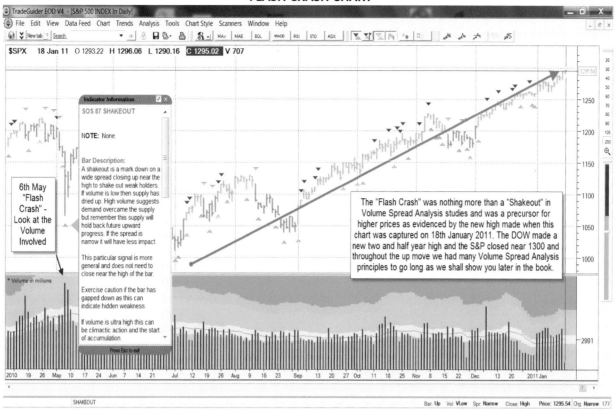

As you can see on the Flash Crash Chart, what we witnessed on that May 6th was a giant *Shakeout* of the market. The Smart Money operators were expecting higher prices and wanted to catch all the stops before moving the price up. They were bullish and stocks were going to rise. Of course they wanted to buy at the best possible price. Wouldn't you do the same? Buy at the lowest price knowing you could sell it later for much more than what you bought it for? That is the game on Wall Street. Buy low, sell high. Be a predator, a clever predator that understands exactly how the prey think and act. It is like herding sheep, steering them, rounding them up, and then placing them in a pen.

Whether we admit it or not, human beings are conditioned to act as a herd and the media unwittingly play a key role in helping investors and traders form an opinion about traded instruments such as stocks, commodities, futures, or even forex. Like a twisted version of mass hysteria, when media-induced opinions about traded instruments are wrong and the majority of the uninformed Herd believes them, it will cost them dearly. Smart Money players know how you will act as an investor or trader. They know how to steer you. They know the two most powerful human emotions are greed and fear, and those emotions are our worst enemies when it comes to making investment or trading decisions.

As Mark Twain once said, "If you do not read the newspaper, you are uninformed, and if you do read the newspaper, you are misinformed."

Later in this book we will examine why markets tend to do the opposite of what any normal person would expect. We will look at why British Petroleum stock was a great buy on June 25th, 2010 when the oil spill crisis in the Gulf of Mexico was at its worst and the rumors of British Petroleum going out of business were rife. I will also show you how to identify professional buying (the Smart Money activity) on a price chart.

You will be able to recognize and profit from buying at the right price, despite the bad news and rumors all around you. You will know when not to buy (or go short) when all the news is good. For an example, we will examine the US stock JP Morgan by looking at great earnings reports and fundamentals, which would create public expectation of higher prices, but then show an immediate drop in the stock price (which actually occurred)!

So you may ask, "Is market manipulation a good thing or a bad thing?"

Well, I feel that if you can read a chart correctly, then the volatility caused when markets are 'moved' is a very good thing. When you become an educated chart reader, you can see with clarity the intentions of the manipulators, thus trade in harmony with what's happening.

You may also wonder, "Are the market manipulators evil beings that have intent on stealing your money?"

I do not believe so. These are clever individuals who understand human nature and market structure. Like most that are successful in any endeavor, they view their activity as a game and have acquired the knowledge and practiced skills required to win. Like prosperous poker players, they simply take advantage of opportunities that arise in certain situations. These individuals have the financial supremacy and understanding of the financial markets. They have an edge over the retail investor or trader and use this to their advantage to make profits and gain for their own accounts.

At this point you may be thinking, "Why is this chapter relevant to making money in the markets? Why can't we just go straight to the charts and all the set-ups?"

Well, the reason it is vital and important to know this information is because in order to *win* the game, you must first accept it exists and understand it. The average retail trader who does not accept this reality calls to mind another poker maxim: If you sit down at the table and do not know who the patsy is- you're the patsy.

I did not initially accept this as reality when I first met Tom, but as I began to examine the financial markets closely, I noticed consistent patterns. The charts always appeared to be at odds with what was on television and what was reported in the financial press. Later, I will show you two things that both confirmed my thoughts and increased my interest in the teachings of Tom Williams and his methodology of Volume Spread Analysis.

On December 22nd, 2006 a video was produced and uploaded to YouTube. It became very controversial and many attempts were made to remove it from the public domain. This video was an interview with the host of CNBC's *Mad Money*, Jim Cramer. He is also a bestselling author and former hedge fund manager, as well as being the co-founder and chairperson of www.TheStreet.com, an American financial news and services website. In this video, Cramer reveals how he was able to influence prices of several stocks, including Apple and Rimm (of Blackberry fame). Below is a partial transcript of the interview verbatim of Jim Cramer on *Wall Street Confidential* Dec. 22nd, 2006. I have put in bold the parts that will be interesting for you to note (the full interview is available on www.youtube.com):

*You know, a lot of times when I was short at my Hedge Fund—when I was positioned short, meaning I needed it down—**I would create a level of activity beforehand that could drive the futures**. It doesn't take much money. Similarly, if I were long and I wanted to make things a little bit rosy, I would go in and take a bunch of stocks and make sure that they're higher. Maybe commit $5 million in capital, and I could affect it. What you're seeing now is maybe it is probably a bigger market. Maybe you need $10 million in capital to knock the stuff down.*

But it is a fun game, and it is a lucrative game. You can move it up and then fade it—that often creates a very negative feel. So let's say you take a longer term view intraday and you say, 'Listen, I'm going to boost the futures, and the when the real sellers come in—the real market comes in—they're going to knock it down and that is going to create a negative view.' That is a strategy very worth doing when you're valuing on a day-to-day basis. I would encourage anyone who's in the hedge fund game to do it- because it is legal and a very quick way to make money... and very satisfying.

By the way, no one else in the world would ever admit that. But I do not care, and I'm not going to say that on TV.

In the next section of the interview, Cramer is discussing what struggling hedge funds do to improve their performances before the end of the year.

It is really vital these next six days because of your payday; you've really got to control the market. You can't let it lift. When you get a Research in Motion, (RIMM) it is really important to use a lot of your firepower to knock that down, because it is the fulcrum of the market today. So, let's say I was short. What I would do is I would hit a lot of guys with RIMM.

Now you can't 'foment'. That is a violation. You can't create an impression that a stock's down. But you do it anyway because the SEC doesn't understand it. That is the only sense that I would say is illegal. But a hedge fund that'd not up a lot really has to do a lot now to save itself.

This is different from what I was talking about at the beginning where I was talking about buying the QQQs and stuff. This is actually blatantly illegal. But when you have six days and your company may be in doubt because you're down, I think it is really important to foment—if I were one of these guys—foment an impression that Research in Motion (RIMM) is not any good because Research in Motion (RIMM) is the key today.

Cramer goes on to talk about the actual mechanics of what one would do to knock Research in Motion down. Then he continues:

*If I wanted it to go higher, I would take and bid, take and bid, take and bid, and if I wanted it to go lower, I'd hit and offer, hit and offer, hit and offer. And I could get a stock like RIMM for maybe—that might cost me $15 to $20 million to knock RIM down—**but it would be fabulous because it would beleaguer all the moron longs who are also keying on Research in Motion.***

*So we're seeing that. Again, when your company is in survival mode, it is really important to defeat Research in Motion, and get the Pisanis of the world and people talking about it as if there's something wrong with RIMM. **Then you would call the Journal and you would get the Bozo reporter on Research in Motion and you would feed that Palm's got a killer that is going to give away. These are all the things you must do in a day like today, and if you're not doing it, then maybe you shouldn't be in the game.***

Cramer describes in considerable detail about how if he were to short Apple's stock today, he would knock Apple's stock down. Then he says:

What's important when you're in that hedge fund mode is to not do anything remotely truthful... because truth is so against view that it is important to create a new truth to develop a fiction.

A minute later, when talking about how company fundamentals do not matter, Cramer says:

The great thing about the market is it has nothing to do with the actual stocks. *Now, maybe two weeks from now, the buyers will come to their senses and realize that everything that they heard was a lie, but then again, Fannie Mae lied about their earnings for $6 billion, so there's just fiction and fiction and fiction.*

I think it is important for people to recognize that the way that the market really works is to have that nexus of hit the brokerage houses with a series of orders that can push it down, then leak it to the press, and then get it on CNBC—that is also very important. And then you have a kind of a vicious cycle down. It is a pretty good game. It can pay for a percentage or two.

On March 12th, 2009 Jim Cramer's YouTube video came back to haunt him as excerpts were finally played on national television. It wasn't on the financial networks as one would expect, but these excerpts were played on Comedy Central in an excellent interview on *The Daily Show with Jon Stewart.* Jon Stewart is well known in the United States for being a hard hitter and not mincing words.

In the following dialogue, 'JS' stands for John Stewart and 'JC' stands for Jim Cramer. They use the word 'shenanigans' to describe the manipulation. Call it by a different name- it is all the same thing:

JS: How the hell did we end up here, Mr. Cramer? What happened?

JC: I do not know. I do not know- big fan of the show. Who's never said that?

JS: Well, many people. Let me just explain to you very quickly one thing that is somewhat misinterpreted. This was not directed at you, per say. I just want you to know that. We threw some banana cream pies at CNBC. Obviously, you got some schmutz on your jacket from it.

JC: I think that everyone could come under criticism from it. I mean, we all should have seen it more. I mean, admittedly this is a terrible one. Everyone got it wrong. I got a lot of things wrong because I think it was kind of one in a million shot. But I do not think anyone should be spared in this environment.

JS: So, then, if I may, why were you mad at us? (Audience laughs)

JC: No-

JS: Because I was under the impression that you thought we were being unfair.

JC: No, you have my friend Joe Nasair and Joe called me and said, "Jim, do I need to apologize to you?" and I said, "No". We're fair game. We're big network. We've been out front. We've made mistakes. We have 17 hours of live TV a day to do. But I—

JS: Maybe you could cut down on that. (Audience laughs) *So let me tell you why I think this has caused some attention. It is the gap between what CNBC advertises itself as and what it is and the help that people need to discern this. Let me show you... This is the promo for your show.*

JC: Okay.

-The "In Cramer We Trust" promo is played-

JS: Is not that- you know, look, we are both snake oil salesmen to a certain extent...

JC: I'm not discerning...

JS: But we do label the show as snake oil here. Is not there a problem with selling snake oil and labeling it as vitamin tonic and saying that it cures impetigo etc. etc. etc. Is not that the difficulty here?

JC: I think that there are two kinds of people. People come out and make good calls and bad calls that are financial professionals and there are people who say they only make good calls and they are liars. I try really hard to make as many good calls as I can.

JS: I think the difference is not good call/bad call. The difference is real market and unreal market. Let me show you. This is... you ran a hedge fund-

JC: Yes I did.

-The December 22, 2006 video is played-
(Cramer says, "You know a lot of times when I was short at my hedge fund and I was position short, meaning I needed it down, I would create a level of activity beforehand that could drive the futures. It doesn't take much money.")

JS: What does that mean?

JC: Okay, this was a just a hyperbolic example of what people— You had a great piece about short selling earlier.

JS: Yes, I was—

JC: I have been trying to reign in short selling, trying to expose what really happens. This is what goes on. What I'm trying to say is I didn't do this, but I'm trying to explain to people these are the shenanigans that—

JS: Well, it sounded as if you were talking about that you had done it.

JC: Then I was inarticulate because I did-- I barely traded the futures. Let me say this: I am trying to expose this stuff. Exactly what you guys do and I am trying to get the regulators to look at it.

JS: That is very interesting because... roll 2:10!

-The 2:10 video is played-
(The YouTube video was discussed earlier.)

JC: It is on TV now.

JS: I want the Jim Cramer on CNBC to protect me from that Jim Cramer.

JC: I think the way you do that is to show—Okay, the regulators watch the tape they realize the shenanigans that go on, they can go after this. Now, they did catch Madoff, that is a shame.

JS: Now why when you talk about the regulators, why not the financial news networks? That is the whole point of this? CNBC could be an incredibly powerful tool of illumination for people that believe that there are two markets: One that has been sold to us as long term. Put your money in 401Ks. Put your money in pensions and just leave it there. Do not worry about it. It is all doing fine. Then, there's this other market; this real market that is occurring in the back room. Where giant piles of money are going in and out and people are trading them and it is transactional and it is fast. But it is dangerous, it is ethically dubious and it hurts the long-term market. So what it feels like to us—and I'm talking purely as a layman—it feels like we are capitalizing your adventure by our pension and our hard earned money. And that it is a game that you know, that you know is going on! But that you go on television as a financial network and pretend is not happening.

JC: Okay. First, my first reaction is absolutely we could do better. Absolutely, there are shenanigans and we should call them out. Everyone should. I should do a better job at it. But my second thing is, I talk about the shorts every single night. I got people in Congress who I've been working with trying to get the uptick rule. It is a technical thing but it would cut down a lot of the games that you are talking about. I'm trying. I'm trying. Am I succeeding? I'm trying.

JS: But the gentleman on that video is a sober, rational individual. And the gentleman on 'Mad Money' is throwing plastic cows through his legs and shouting, "Sell! Sell! Sell!" And then coming on two days later and going, "I was wrong. You should have bought…" Like- I can't reconcile the brilliance and knowledge that you have of the intricacies of the market with the crazy **bullsh**** you do every night! That is English. That is treating people like adults.

JC: How about if I try it?

JS: Try what?

JC: Try doing that. I'll try that.

JS: That would be great, but it is not just you. It is larger forces at work. It is this idea that the financial news networks are not just guilty of a sin of omission but a sin of commission- they are in bed with them.

JC: No, we're not in bed with them. Come on. I do not think that is fair. Honestly. I think that we try to report the news and I think that people—

JS: A couple of guys do. This guy Faber…

JC: He's fabulous, Faber.

JS: And maybe two other guys…

JC: He's fabulous and he's done some things that have really blown the cover off a lot of stuff.

JS: But this thing was ten years in the making!

JC: Right.

JS: And it is not going to be fixed tomorrow. But the idea that you could have on the guys from Bear Sterns and Merrill Lynch, and guys that had leveraged 35 to 1…

JC: I know.

JS: And then blame mortgage holders. I mean- that is insane.

JC: I never did that... I'm sorry you're absolutely right. I always wish that people would swear themselves in before they came on the show. I've had a lot of CEO's lie to me on the show. It is very painful. I do not have subpoena power.

JS: But do not—you're pretending that you are a doe-eyed innocent. Watch. Roll. I mean, if I may...

JC: It is your show for heaven's sake.

JS: Roll 2:12.

JC: No! Not 2:12!

-The 2:12 video is played-
(This is the other part of the YouTube video discussed above. Note how Cramer is not very keen to have this shown on national TV.)

JC: You know...

*JS: I gotta tell you. I understand that you want to make finance entertaining, but it is not a f***ing game. When I watch that I get, I can't tell you how angry it makes me because it says to me you all know. You all know what's going on. You can draw a straight line from those shenanigans to the stuff that was being pulled at Bear and at AIG and all this derivative market stuff that is this weird Wall Street side bet.*

JC: But Jon, do not you want guys like me that have been in it to show the shenanigans? What else can I do? I mean last night's show-

JS: No, no, no, no, no. I want desperately for that, but I feel like that is not what we're getting. What we're getting is... Listen. You knew what the banks were doing and yet were touting it for months and months. The entire network was and is now trying to pretend that this was some sort of crazy, once-in-a-lifetime tsunami that nobody could have seen coming is disingenuous at best and criminal at worst.

JC: But Dick Fogle who ran Lehman Brothers called me in when the stock was at 40 because I thought that the stock was wrong, I thought that it was the wrong place for it to be. He brings me in, lies to me, lies to me, and lies to me. I've known him for twenty years.

JS: The CEO of a company lied to you.

JC: Shocker stock trading.

JS: But is not that financial reporting? What do you think is the role of CNBC?

JC: Look, I have called for star chambers. I want kangaroo courts for these guys. I have not seen any indictments. Where are the indictments? Where are the indictments for AIG? I told the Justice Department, "Here's the way you get the indictment."

JS: It is very easy to get on this after the fact. The measure of the network and the measure of mess- CNBC could act as—No one is asking them to be a regulatory agency, but can't—but whose side are they on? It feels like they have to reconcile as their audience the Wall Street traders that are doing this for constant profit on a day-to-day for short term. These guys' companies were on a Sherman's March through their companies financed by our 401Ks and all the incentives of their companies were for short-term profit. And they burned the f***ing house down with our money and walked away rich as hell and you guys knew that it was going on.

JC: I have a wall of shame. Why do I have banana cream pies- because I throw them at CEO's. Do you know how many times I have pantsed CEOs on my show?

JS: But this is not, as Carly Simon would say, this song ain't about you.

JC: Okay. Alright. You're right. I do not want to personalize it. I think we have reporters who try really hard. We're not always told the truth. But most importantly, the market was going up for a long time and our real sin I think was to believe that it was going to continue to go up a lot in the face of what you just described- a lot of borrowing. A lot of shenanigans and I know I did, I'll bring it up- I didn't think Bear Sterns was going to evaporate overnight. I didn't. I knew the people who ran it. I always thought they were honest. That was my mistake. I really did. I thought they were honest. Did I get taken in because I knew them from before? Maybe to some degree. The guy who came on from Wachovia was an old friend of mine who helped hire me.

JS: But honest or not, in what world is a 35 to 1 leverage position sane?

JC: The world that made you 30% year after year after year beginning from 1999 to 2007 and it became—

JS: But is not that part of the problem? Selling this idea that you do not have to do anything- anytime you sell people the idea that sit back and you'll get 10 to 20 percent on your money, do not you always know that it is going to be a lie? When are we going to realize in this country that our wealth is work? That we're workers and by selling this idea that of, "Hey man, I'll teach you how to be rich." How is that any different than an infomercial?

JC: Well, I think that your goal should always be to try to expose the fact that there is no easy money. I wish I had found Madoff.

JS: But there are literally shows called "Fast Money".

JC: I think that people... There's a market for it and you give it to them.

JS: There's a market for cocaine and hookers. What is the responsibility of the people who cover Wall Street? Who are you responsible to? The people with the 401Ks and the pensions and the general public or the Wall Street traders, and by the way this casts an aspersion on all of Wall Street when I know that is unfair as well. The majority of those guys are working their a***s off. They're really bright guys. I know a lot of them. They're just trying to do the right thing and they're getting f***ed in the ass, too.

JC: True. True. I think as a network we produce a lot of interviews where I think that we have been—there have been people who have not told the truth. Should we have been constantly pointing out the mistakes that were made? Absolutely- I truly wish we had done more. I think that we have been very tough on the previous Treasury Secretary, very tough on the previous administration how they didn't get it, very tough on Ben Bernanke. But at the same time...

JS: But he's the guy who wrote the rule that allowed people to over-leverage.

JC: I trash him every night. I've called him a liar on TV. What am I going to do? Should we all call him liars? I'm a commentator. We have—and you can take issues with the fact that I throw bulls and bears and I can still be considered serious. I'm not Eric Sevareid. I'm not Edward R. Morrow. I'm a guy trying to do an entertainment show about business for people to watch. But it is difficult to have a reporter to say I just came from an interview with Hank Wilson and he lied his darn fool head off. It is difficult. I think it challenges the boundaries.

JS: Yeah. I'm under the assumption, and maybe this is purely ridiculous, but I'm under the assumption that you do not just take their word for it at face value. That you actually then go around and try and figure it out. So, again, you now have become the face of this and that is incredibly unfortunate.

JC: I wish I had done a better job trying to figure out the 30 to 1 and whether it was going to blow up. It did. Once it did I, was late in saying it was bad.

JS: So maybe we could remove the financial expert and the "In Cramer We Trust" and start getting back to fundamentals on reporting, as well, and I can go back to making fart noises and funny faces.

JC: I think we make that deal right here.

-End of Interview-

On November 28th, 2010 on MSNBC's online US business report, I read an article headlined *"Everyday Investors Wonder if Market is Rigged"*. This report was the most interesting article I have ever seen in mainstream media. In it, authors Bernard Condon, Pallavi Gogoi, and Rachel Beck says:

The Wall Street insider trading investigation may lead everyday investors – already rattled by a stock market meltdown, a one day Flash Crash, and the Madoff scandal – to finally conclude that the game is rigged.

"Virtually everyone on the Street believes there are significant improprieties, and I think there is an even more important point for the massive number of investors who are not Wall Street players," says former New York Gov. Eliot Spitzer, once known as the "sheriff of Wall Street" for aggressively prosecuting white-collar crime as state attorney general. "And that is for most of us, you can't beat these guys at their own game."

Some pros on Wall Street say hesitation by small investors is good news. It means that there's plenty of "dry powder" to propel the market higher in the next few months when and if the little guy finally relents and joins in the rally.

The record for hedge funds hasn't been so impressive, either. Since 2008, when the number of those funds hit ten thousand, nearly three thousand have gone out of business, according to Hedge Fund Research in Chicago.

In addition, "The edge is hugely exaggerated," says Richard Ferri, an advocate of low-cost index funds and founder of the investment advisory firm, Portfolio Solutions, "If the small investor 'does the right thing', he can do 99% better than anyone else."

I totally agree with Mr. Ferri. If the small investor can do the right thing, then there is a good chance that he or she can be successful. In my opinion, doing the right thing starts by learning what the game is and then learning how to read supply and demand imbalances as they appear on the charts, as well as following a few simple rules.

So are the retail traders and investors finally waking up to the true mechanics of the markets? And if so, can they take advantage of market manipulation?

I would say that depends on the individual. By reading this book, you are already on your way to recognizing great trading and investing opportunities. We do not really need to be concerned about the 'why, what, if, and, or but's of the market, but we do need to be thinking and acting in harmony with the Smart Money. To do so will involve a little bit of research and effort on your part to act, think, and react like a predator, not the prey- and that is what I am going to teach you in this book.

There is public material readily available on the subject of market manipulation, so I won't dwell on that subject any longer. The markets have been the same for hundreds of years and they are very unlikely to change in the future. Lots of information and useful tips are available at *www.marketmanipulation.com*. This site condenses much of the public information on the Internet. I highly suggest you visit the site with an open mind and decide for yourself. We all have different belief systems, but I recommend you use your mind like a parachute because it is only best used when you open it!

CHAPTER 3
The Smart Money and the Not-So-Smart Money

In Chapter 2, we analyzed the mechanics of the financial markets and now we are going to look at some of the common pitfalls experienced by many traders and investors of different skill levels that cause losses. Remember that 3,000 hedge funds went out of business in 2008-2009, so even the big players can get it wrong.

However, when you can read the imbalances of supply and demand in any time frame or market, money can be made when the market is moving up or down (although, it can be a little more difficult to read when the market moves sideways, as I will show you).

In Tom Williams' two books, *"The Undeclared Secrets That Drive the Stock Market"* and *"Master the Markets"*, **Tom refers to the Not-So-Smart Money as the Herd**. Now let's examine the actual definition of what a herd is and how that can be applied to the financial markets:

Herd [hurd] *noun: 1. A large group of animals, especially hoofed mammals, 2. (Derogatory): a large group of people, typically with a shared characteristic*

Interestingly, the dictionary term shows a herd of people as derogatory, but in fact, as Tom explained to me, human beings often act as a herd. A great example that I have observed, not only in Chicago where I live, but also all over the world, is when a store has a markdown sale. As you may know, 'Black Friday' in the USA is when retail stores offer the biggest discounts on the first Friday after Thanksgiving.

Hundreds and sometimes thousands of people wait, even camp out for 2 days, just for stores to open at 5:00am or earlier. People go through this trouble just to get a bargain! Supposedly, they want to feel good about saving money and making a great purchase.

So what happens when the doors open at 5:00am? Most often than not, the crowd stampedes like a herd to rush to the items they want, in fear that someone else may take the cherished items and there will be none left. In fact, in 2008 a Wal-Mart security guard was killed in a stampede on Black Friday in Long Island, New York. The New York Times headline was *"Wal-Mart Worker Trampled to Death by Frenzied Black Friday Shoppers"*.

How does this apply to trading and investing? Simple- the very emotions experienced by those wanting to get the bargain prices are the same emotions as those experienced by almost every human who trades the markets.

However, the group we call the Smart Money are very intelligent and they fully understand the underlying reasons why people buy and sell at certain times. Also, the Smart Money understands what members of the Herd base their decisions on. Whilst providing educational seminars and live trading events on my travels around the world, I have met thousands of retail traders and investors. I find that there are 5 main analytical tools (and I use that term loosely) that the Herd use to trade and make their investments.

I can assure you that these forms of analysis are the reason so few retail traders and investors make money in the markets:

- Technical analysis using back tested past price analysis and formulas.

- Recommendations from television, newspapers, brokers etc.

- Fundamental analysis especially when expert analysts suggest an instrument will move a certain direction (we will examine this more closely in a moment).

- 'Black Box' software systems and trading robots that promise guarantees of riches by giving buy and sell signals. According to the advertising and marketing claims, they allegedly produce amazing results with guaranteed percentage returns.

- Tips received through email, Facebook, Twitter, and other social media sources. Unless these are from a very trusted and proven source, beware!

There are two facts that I learned early on as I began my journey as a VSA expert, which have served me well whenever I analyze the markets:

1. The chart never lies.

2. The past price does not move the future price.

In order to prove these two facts, we will examine the crude oil charts of 2008. Many of you will remember that the gas/petrol prices skyrocketed around the world and oil was supposedly in scarce supply. Some of the world's top oil analysts were predicting a price of $200 a barrel! It's ironic that two years later, the BP spill happened causing many scientists to express their concern that the oil well would gush indefinitely.

Now let's take a look at what actually happened. You can see for yourself just how influenced one becomes when you see and hear information that all points in one direction. In this case, oil was to go to $200 a barrel and many traders, investors, and indeed, even airlines got caught on the wrong side of the oil market because they did not know what the chart was telling them. But as a soon-to-be VSA expert, you will know better in the future!

News Article 1. An Oracle of Oil Predicts $200-a-Barrel Crude, by Louise Story, New York Times May 21st, 2011:

Arjun N. Murti remembers the pain of the oil shocks of the 1970s. But he is bracing for something far worse now: He foresees a "super spike" — a price surge that will soon drive crude oil to $200 a barrel.

Mr. Murti, 39, argues that the world's seemingly unquenchable thirst for oil means prices will keep rising from here and stay above $100 into 2011. Others disagree, arguing that prices could abruptly tumble if speculators in the market rush for the exits. But the grim calculus of Mr. Murti's prediction issued in March and reconfirmed two weeks ago, is enough to give anyone pause: in an America of $200 oil, gasoline could cost more than $6 a gallon.

(See the complete article by visiting www.nytimes.com)

"An Oracle of Oil Predicts $200-a-barrel Crude" was published May 21st, 2008, exactly 3 weeks before supply and selling came in heavily, as we shall see. The chart never lies. The weekly oil futures using TradeGuider RT software with Volume Spread Analysis signals

VSA CHART 1

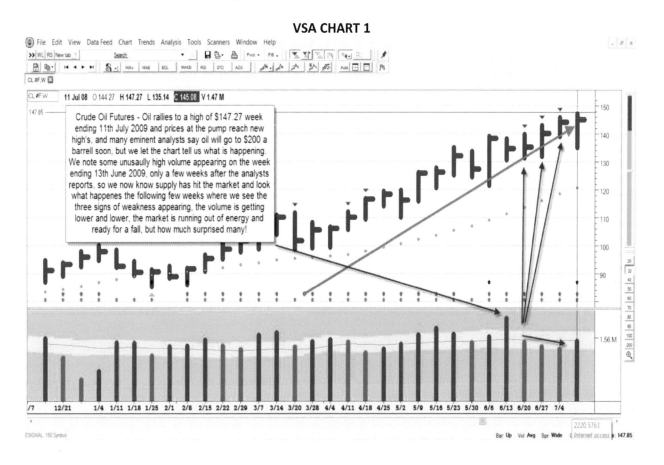

Looking at the week ending on June 13th, 2008 we can see that unusually high Volume appears on **VSA CHART 1** and the Spread of the bar on that week is very narrow. On the daily chart (not shown), we had a signal appear called *The End of a Rising Market* in the TradeGuider software. Combined with the signals that appeared, the following three weeks convinced me that this market was being sold on all this bullish news.

I decided to post my analysis on YouTube. I warned viewers of the weakness and impending fall of oil (this is still viewable on YouTube and I want to point out that this was posted in foresight, not hindsight). I received hundreds of abusive emails questioning my analysis. I was criticized for not being a famous analyst, as well as scoffed at to dare question the mainstream media reports! I was ridiculed from many circles, but I had faith in my chart reading skills. I was subsequently vindicated as oil prices plummeted to around $34.00 a barrel.

On **VSA CHART 1**, examine the three bars with the Volume Spread Analysis signals (look at the red triangles at the top, pointed out by the three red arrows shown).

Note that as the market prices are rising, the Volume is falling week by week. Only one thing can cause this fall in Volume and that is the lack of interest in higher prices by the Smart Money players. They had already started selling in the prior weeks! The logic is that if they are not participating, we will see low Volume and in the TradeGuider software we refer to this scenario as *No Demand at a Market Top*.

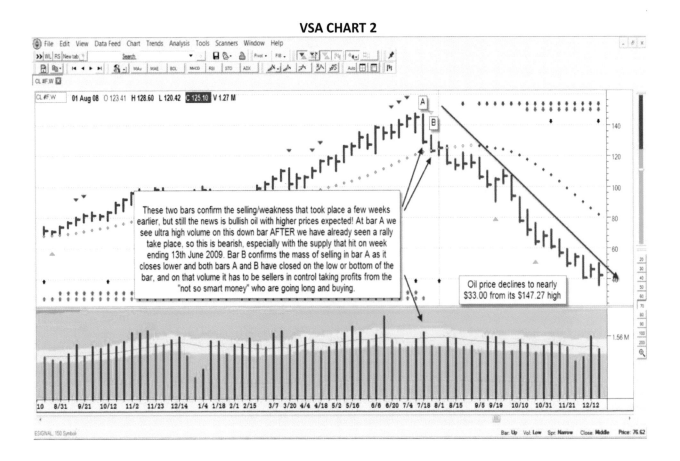

At bars A and B on **VSA CHART 2**, we now see the true confirmation of the weakness that has appeared in the background. By background we mean the previous number of bars that indicate the market price action, which will either be bullish or bearish, or what I refer to as weak or strong.

Due to the observed weakness, it is at this point we would start to consider shorting the market. **It is imperative to remember that we want to short the market when the down-trend is confirmed - not before.** The TradeGuider software has three very simple trending systems that show this and I will explain that in detail later in Chapter 11 – *"Some Basic Volume Spread Analysis Trade Set-ups Explained"*.

As you look at **VSA CHART 2**, you can see these trending systems where the down-trend is confirmed by the red bars, the red diamonds, as well as the red, pink, and black arrows above the bars (these are proprietary tools incorporated in the TradeGuider software. The tools are available as an add-on study within the TradeGuider portfolio of products.)

If you had been using any type of technical analysis that examined past price in an attempt to predict the future price of the charts shown, you may as well have accepted that oil would be going to $200 a barrel. Past price analysis tools by their very nature are lagging (e.g. MACD, Stochastics, and RSI). They are not leading edge indicators and they were giving multiple buying signals at $147.00 because the price was rising and we also had exceeded many of the standard moving average periods, such as 20 day M/A, which made the trends bullish. The news from the analysts confirmed everything you were seeing on the technical charts.

However, once you are able to correctly read and analyze supply and demand from the charts, you can combine Volume Spread Analysis with your current technical and fundamental analysis. By doing so, you are giving yourself a trading edge which will enable you to make intelligent, informed, and hopefully more profitable trading decisions. **It is possible to observe the intent of the Smart Money.**

Many of our most successful customers have combined VSA with their current trading style and methods of analysis. Although, we have come to notice that there are many who have set aside much of what they have previously learned in order to focus solely on the Volume Spread Analysis methodology.

It is important to remember, that when the Smart Money players start selling, they will sell as prices rise! This confuses many uninformed traders and investors that have been haring the good news while waiting on the sidelines. What they do is jump onto the 'rising price bandwagon' (a.k.a. suckers rally), only to get hammered by the effect of the Smart Money's prior selling positions, which results in the price 'dropping off the cliff'.

This causes embarrassed bandwagon buyers to either get out of their trades at break-even, or suffer the pain of losses as stops are hit. This is known as **stop hunting**. This phase, by its nature and intent, effectively creates profits for the Smart Money and marks the price back down. This creates the scenario for more buying (if they are bullish) or heavy selling, as seen in the crude oil examples that mark the market top.

Remember that by its very nature, every bar contains a combination of buying *and* selling. **The art of reading the chart becomes a combination of individual bar Volume analysis, as well as the analysis of the background bars.** Combining the two analysis helps you come to the conclusion as to the intent of the parties involved in creating the current *and* background bars. It is this concept that many traders find difficult to understand, but once grasped, your reward will be that the chart will come alive in front of your eyes!

Reading this book, absorbing its knowledge, and examining Volume very closely by paying attention to ultra high and ultra low Volume, you can become a Smart Money trader and investor yourself and avoid the costly pitfalls experienced by the Not-So-Smart Money.

Always remember that chart reading is a skill that develops over time, much like learning to play golf or a musical instrument.

I would do an experiment. What I found helpful was taking screenshots of an individual stock or commodity. When I saw news about that particular instrument, I would look for unusual Volume, wait six months, and revisit that chart and news story only to be amazed. Most of the time, the instrument did the very opposite of what technical analysis was predicting and what the fundamental analysis was suggesting. The actions of the instrument confirmed my gut instincts, as well as what I had seen as a result of carefully studying the Price, the Spread, and the Volume.

After consistent findings with this 'experiment', I knew I had to write this book and follow in the footsteps of my great mentors, Richard Demille Wyckoff and Tom Williams. I had a passion to attempt to help even the odds for the everyday trader and investor that wanted to succeed and make it in the markets.

You can make it in the markets and be successful, but you will need to embrace the paradigm shift of Volume Spread Analysis in your thinking and trading toolset. We can provide plenty of tools that can help you make those necessary shifts in your belief system, but as I stated before, that is only if *you* are open minded and look at the evidence. It is all right in front of your eyes- all you need to do is read the chart!

CHAPTER 4
Beware of the News!

In Chapter 3, we discussed the Smart Money players and how they take full advantage of understanding crowd behavior. Now, let's look at two case studies. Both case studies will be explained in more details later in the book, but for now, we will focus on some very simple principles that everyone can understand.

Remember what Mark Twain said, "If you do not read the newspaper, you are uninformed, if you do read the newspaper, you are misinformed."

When I first met Tom, he described an incident in which the trading syndicate he worked for wanted to accumulate, or buy more shares, in a particular stock they had been following. In order to do so, the syndicate needed to create a level of activity beforehand to convey the impression the stock had problems.

Tom and some members of the syndicate had been planted in the annual general meeting of Teledyne, the company in question. There were inquiries that gave a false impression that the stock might be in trouble. The rumors concerned a lost contract that never actually existed, but it was enough to start the snowball rolling. The day after the annual general meeting, the circulating news was negative and the syndicate sold just enough stock to cause a selling panic. As the stock began to fall, they knew they would be getting a bargain. The stock was now at a very attractive price, so they began to buy at lower prices.

This is why the following two rules are very important in your learning:

1. Weakness appears on an up bar

2. Strength appears on a down bar

Rule 1. Weakness Appears on an Up Bar

In a rising market, or when a market has broken out of a sideways range and weakness appears (a selling short opportunity) on the chart, it will appear on an **up bar**, which is a price bar that has closed higher than the previous bar. This will be on unusually high Volume by such comparison. TradeGuider will indicate this as ultra high Volume.

If the opposite occurs (unusually low Volume), TradeGuider will show it as ultra low Volume (the Spread could be telltale narrower than previous bars).

At first glance, that may appear as though I am contradicting myself by stating that weakness will appear on high Volume (or preferably, ultra high) and then also on low Volume (or ultra low) on up bars, but the statement is factually correct! So, why is this?

The answer is simple. When the Smart Money players begin to dump their holdings of whatever instrument is being traded (stocks, futures, forex, commodities etc.) and their sell orders are all coming in one after another, *that creates the* ultra high Volume. This is what is called the **distribution phase** indicated by *Supply Overcoming Demand*. An analogy of this is in the retail environment where manufacturers who have goods to sell supply them to retail 'distributors'.

In this situation, sellers are overcoming buyers at a certain price level, or range (this is often seen at previous resistance levels). Now after this activity has taken place, the market will often move sideways and not suddenly collapse because the Smart Money need to ensure that all their sell orders are being satisfied. This explains why the distribution phase can take time. Another indication of this lack of interest on the part of the Smart Money is that it causes the price to peak and roll over in a characteristic mushroom-like shape, which is easy to spot.

The Smart Money ensures that the price is held at a certain level by buying some of it back to trap and encourage the uninformed Herd to enter into or remain in long trades. They will often be lured into this, after seeing the frenzy of what they *think* is buying. They assume this is the case due to the high Volume and rising prices, but it is the exact opposite of what is actually happening!

The time to short the market is when price starts confirming the lack of buying interest and begins to rollover and trend down (I will show specific set-ups later that will amplify this principle in greater detail).

VSA CHART 3

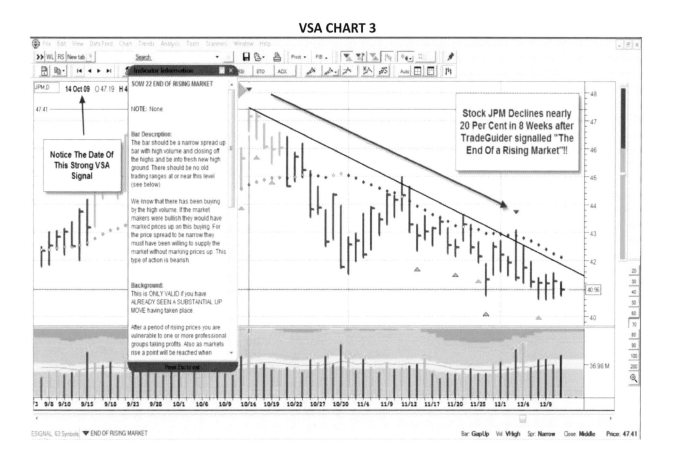

TradeGuider **VSA CHART 3** is a daily chart of US stock, JP Morgan Chase, with an indicator signal that appears in the TradeGuider software program called End of a Rising Market. Note that the date of the signal is the 14th of October 2009, which is very significant as we shall see. This stock had been in a strong bull run since early March 2009. In fact, on March 6th 2009 the stock was heavily accumulated and bought at the low of $15.52, which was the start of the up-trend.

Looking at **VSA CHART 3**, notice that in the trend we see an unfolding pattern with up bars with extremely low Volume, or at least lower than the previous two bars.

If you notice, the trend pattern shows price progressing upwards. The Smart Money will withdraw their interest because they have already sold and made a nice profit. This confirms that they have no intention of buying since prior bars confirm market weakness. This contradicts the strength that the news media will most likely be reporting.

On the 14th of October the stock gaps up on ultra high Volume and a very narrow Spread bar. Price can also range, or channel over a number of bars. On **VSA CHART 3**, October 14th, 2009, this stock is getting heavily distributed (sold) by the Smart Money that will have bought this stock at much lower prices. Remember, the end game is profit!

At the October 14th bar, we observe that the stock has gapped up, which is unusual activity in its own right, and closes at a new high of $46.90. We have now made new highs with no price action in the past at this level for at least 500 bars. We call this **Fresh New Ground**. Take note of the following:

- Increased massive Volume over previous bars.

- The Spread of the bar is narrow, not wide (in fact, the high of the daily bar on the 14th of October 2009 is at $47.20, the low is $46.37).

- The Closing Price is near the middle at $46.90.

If all that Volume was the Smart Money buying at this level, you would expect a wider Spread on the bar and a Closing Price up, or near the high of the bar(s), but this is not what we are seeing.

What we are actually seeing is *The End of a Rising Market* and there is a specific way to trade this. If we look closely at the simple logic of what is happening on this bar, then we must surely conclude the following:

- **Volume:** Smart Money players clearly appear active as seen in the massive Volume shown at the bottom of the chart (represented by the green bar. Note: there is no significance to the color of the bar for the purposes of this explanation, so ignore the fact its green because coloring is a proprietary element of the TradeGuider software program).

- **Spread:** The Spread of the bar is extremely narrow and the Volume is high. Most likely, and more often than not, the Herd will be rushing in and buying. The Smart Money will satisfy every buy order with a sell order and say, "Thanks very much you mugs!" as they take in more profit since the have bought much lower!

- **Closing Price:** The Closing Price is very important here, too. It closes near the middle of the bar on that narrow range.

We have ultra high Volume with a narrow Spread bar, closing in the middle and we are into fresh high ground. What could be causing this ultra high Volume? Both buyers and sellers are interacting at this level and the buyers are the Herd, or the Not-So-Smart Money and the sellers are the Smart Money. The Smart Money people have now made a tidy profit and unloaded their positions. They made this stock a weak stock with this tactic and they know it.

Why October 14th? Why not sell a week before or even two weeks before?

Surely they would still have made a nice profit. Timing is everything and the Smart Money players know this. Plus, they have information that the retail traders and investors do not have. Look at the news about this stock on October 14th for a clue. We see in the News Article 2 that there is a very bullish earnings report.

News Article 2. JPMorgan Scores Big in Latest Quarter, by Davis Elis, CNNMoney.com May 1st, 2011:

JPMorgan Chase delivered its strongest performance since the financial crisis first took hold two years ago, as the company reported earnings on Wednesday that towered above Wall Street's expectations.

The bank's quarterly profits were driven largely by a strong performance in its investment banking division.

And while losses continued to climb in the consumer-related parts of its business, executives at the company suggested that they were starting to see signs of stability.

(See the complete article by visiting www.CNNMoney.com)

"JP Morgan Scores Big in Latest Quarter" is the headline. The words 'strongest performance' and 'towered above Wall Street's expectations' are used directly below the headline. All the news is bullish. The stock has been going up and up because it is in an up-trend. All technical lagging indicator analysis tools will be firing off buy signals because they track past price to predict future price (and this is a perfect example of why that simply doesn't work. The past price doesn't predict a move of the price in future, and it never will).

It would appear to the Not-So-Smart money that this is a great opportunity to buy this stock because everything they have learned appears to line up:

- The fundamentals look great! *Tick the box!*

- The stock is an up-trend, so if I go long and BUY, I am trading with the trend! *Tick the box!*

- The moving average, Stochastic, MACD, and RSI all give buy signals. *Tick the box!*

- If I do not go into the market and buy now, I will miss the move! *Tick the box!*

Okay, fine- you go ahead and buy, buy, buy, but as you do that, the Smart Money will sell, sell, sell!

The stock will plummet. The Not-So-Smart Money, who now lost their money, rue the day, scratch their heads, throw their computer at the wall, and try to figure out what the hell just happened.

However, when you can read Volume, supply and demand, and the imbalances caused by ultra high and ultra low Volume, you will become a Smart Money trader for yourself! You will be able to study the charts like a professional. You will trade and invest with newly found confidence and vigor because you can clearly see what the true intentions of the Smart Money are and you will be able to trade in harmony with them, not against them.

Could history repeat itself? Would the Smart Money know that the Not-So-Smart Money would fall for the same exact set-up only six months later?

The news reports almost identical price levels, which was acting as resistance, and we get the same result. The stock plummets.

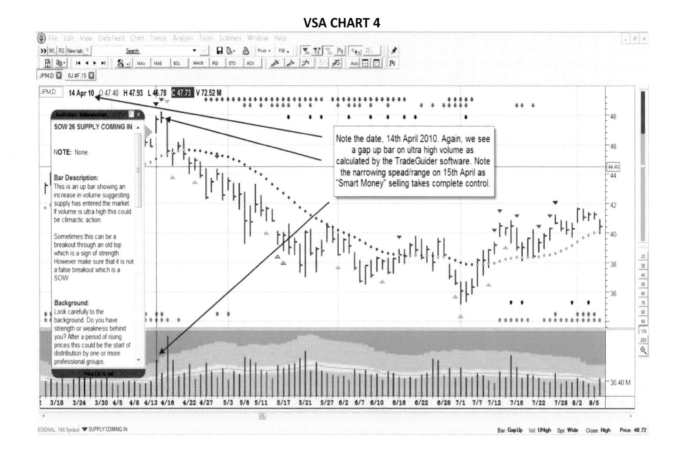

Let's take a look at **VSA CHART 4**. The high on April 14th, 2010 was $47.93 and the high on October 14th, 2009 was $47.20. The low on April 14th, 2010 was $46.78 and the low on Ocotber14[th], 2009 was $46.37. The close on April 14th, 2010 was $47.73 and the close on October 14th 2009 was $46.90.

Was it a coincidence that this stock did this exactly six months after the previous sell off?

Well, you make up your own mind, but you cannot fail to see the excessive Volume on up bars, especially at the previous resistance. Plus, when the news is good and encouraging you to go long, it is a sure sign for you to start looking for a short. Now you have knowledge that hundreds of thousands of traders and investors around the world do not know and may never know, unless of course they find this book or it finds them!

Rule 2. Strength Appears on a Down Bar

When strength, or an opportunity to buy, appears on a chart it will appear on a down bar, which is a price bar that has closed lower than the bar(s) behind it and it will be on unusually high Volume, or unusually low Volume.

As we saw in Rule 1, at first glance it may appear as though I am contradicting myself by stating that strength will appear on high (preferably ultra high) Volume and then also on low (or ultra low) Volume down bars.

This statement is also factually correct! So, once again, why is this?

When the Smart Money professionals begin buying whatever instrument is being traded (stocks, futures, forex, commodities etc.), their buy orders are all coming in one after another and that creates the ultra high Volume. This is what we call the accumulation phase, or *Demand Overcoming Supply*.

To put it simply, buyers are overcoming sellers at a certain price level (this is often seen at previous support levels). After this has taken place, the market will often move sideways and not suddenly rally immediately. This is because the Smart Money needs to ensure all their buy orders are being satisfied and have exhausted all the supply. *This is the reason why the accumulation phase can take time.*

They ensure that the price is held at a certain level by selling back orders to encourage the uninformed traders and investors to go short, which they often will when they have seen the frenzy of what they think is selling. This happens because the price falls and the Volume is very high- they incorrectly assume that the high Volume must be selling.

Time to Buy the Market

The time to buy the market is when we begin to trend up (I will be showing specific set-ups later that explains this principle in more detail). As the trend begins, we see a down bar, or a price bar that has closed lower than the previous bar, and this time the Volume on the down bar is extremely low, or at least lower than the previous two bars.

This tells us that there is no selling pressure or no supply or more sellers, which is an obvious conclusion that the market is going to rally. You must note that even though it is possible to identify market tops and bottoms, do not try and trade them. There are much lower risk entries that take a little more time to develop, so you have to be patient!

A good example of this is the US stock, British Petroleum (BP). I picked this example for many reasons. Tom Williams' signal called *Potential Climactic Action - Sign of Strength 33* is one of the strongest indications that the Smart Money are in the buying process. This signal came up in TradeGuider on June 9th, 2010.

Tom called me and said, "Gavin, I am watching the news and this is horrific... Are we sure that the Volume is correct? It looks very much to me like the big players are piling in and buying BP stock- they must know something we do not. Do you think they have already capped the well and are not telling us?!"

I had no idea what was going on, but I could read the chart. I was due to speak at the Massachusetts Institute of Technology (MIT) in Boston a few weeks after this signal had appeared and I was able to use this as a live example. I had something to show them in foresight and not in hindsight.

When I commenced writing this book in January 2011, the current news then on BP was that their share price had increased. BP's stock price in the US was up from the June 25th, 2010 low of $26.83 to a high as of January 6th, 2011 of $46.60.

BP's stock price had nearly doubled in value in 6 months! During that interim period, the news was so bad that when I spoke at MIT to The Boston Traders Group and they asked me which stock was a good buy at the time, I suggested BP and all they did was laugh probably thinking it was my British sense of humor! I bet no one's laughing now- that was a big opportunity to make money alongside the Smart Money!

You may be saying to yourself, "Well yes, Gavin, it all looks good in hindsight, but what about in foresight?"

That is the wonderful thing about YouTube. I am able to post my analysis as it happens and it is also date stamped. When you get a minute, take a look at TradeGuider's channel at www.youtube.com.

Remember what I said when the oil market was supposed to hit $200 a barrel in 2008 only to get to $147.27 and then plummet to $33.20 in just 6 months?

Beware of the news because all the analysts, including well respected oil analyst Arjun Murti of Goldman Sachs, had warned of an impending oil spike to $200 a barrel barely two months prior to the decline!

I wonder who made profits as the oil market plummeted. Not the airlines, that is for sure, because they were expecting higher prices and therefore hedged accordingly! **Remember, the chart never lies!**

Let's look closely at **VSA CHART 5** and **VSA CHART 6** (BP Daily chart).

VSA CHART 5

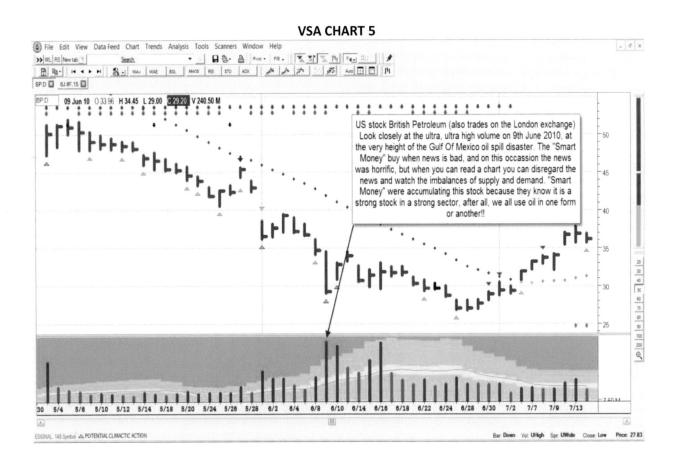

The TradeGuider proprietary signal *Sign of Strength 33* is a powerful indicator. When it appears, as seen on **VSA CHART 6**, it is a clear message from the Smart Money announcing that they are buying everything from the panicking Herd.

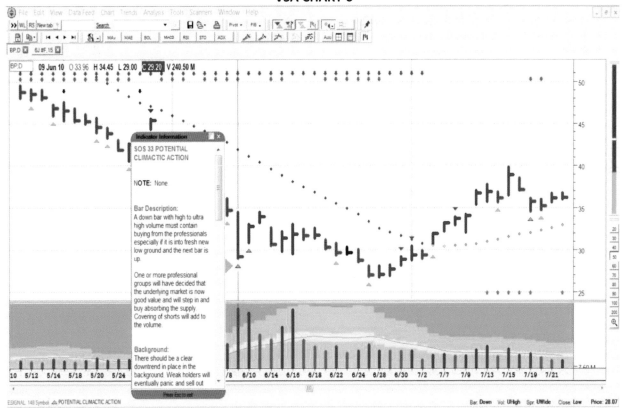

Look at VSA CHART 6. Again, it is a clear message from the Smart Money announcing that they are buying everything from the panicking Herd. We will discuss later the actual place of when to take a long trade later, but even when I see the *Sign of Strength 33* signal, I wait. I do not want to be too hasty since there is still supply (selling) contained in that bar on June 9th, 2010 and that can drive the price lower.

The bar that formed on June 25th, 2010 is extremely significant and forms part 2 of a three-part trade set-up. Let's examine **VSA CHART 7** and the bar that formed on June 25th, 2010.

Firstly, we notice that the Volume is much less than we saw on the 9th and 10th of June, 2010. That is significant because it is shows the selling pressure is getting less and less. This is why the supply (selling) is overcome by the demand (buying) from the Smart Money. More important, however, are the extremely narrow individual bar price Spreads on the 25th and 26th of June, 2010.

If we were to turn the JP Morgan Chart (**VSA CHART 3**) upside down, it would look similar to what you are seeing here. On the JP Morgan chart we observed supply overcoming demand (selling swamping the buying). On the BP chart we see the opposite, demand overcoming supply (buying swamping the selling). This can only mean one outcome - the higher prices we see in all charts and all markets work the same way, including stocks, commodities, futures, currencies and yes, even spot forex!

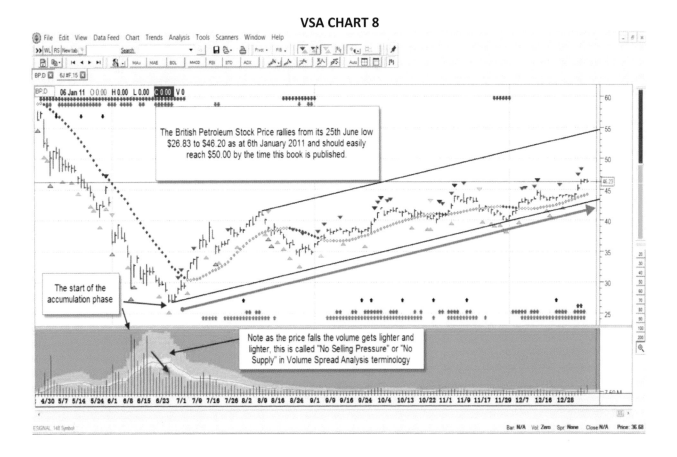

We then see in **VSA CHART 8** the result of the accumulation, namely that demand has overcome supply and higher prices become inevitable. All throughout the up move, the Smart Money is selling some back to bring the price down again in order to *Test for Supply*. In other words, they want to flush out any remaining supply in order to move the price up without having to absorb supply that remains.

If the test is successful, we can expect higher prices especially if the test is on low Volume and there is a narrow Spread down bar into the same area where you first saw the very high Volume. This is a strong buy signal.

However, the news that you hear will almost always be extremely bearish, negative, and fear mongering, which has the effect of blocking your entry into the market at the correct time.

Tom Williams taught me to trust in the chart and nothing else. He also told me that if he had his way, he would lock every retail investor and trader in a dark room with no TV, no newspaper, no outside information or influences, and just get them to trade the VSA principles as they appear.

As Tom says, "If you can read the chart and ignore your natural human instinct to follow the Herd, you can make a lot of money in the markets."

Always look back on previous price action as far as you can to see if there are any unusual Volume areas around support and resistance levels in the background. In **VSA CHART 9**, I looked back 10 years on the monthly BP chart. Stocks move in cycles. Ten years is a cycle. What I found was, as if by magic, clear support around the $27.00 to $30.00 area, exactly where support was found during the Gulf of Mexico oil well disaster.

Again, beware of the news- it is not necessarily that the media reporters are lying; they are simply reporting what they hear and see. Although, I have yet to hear an explanation as to how BP's shares nearly doubled during the worst oil spill crisis America has ever seen, notably when rumors were abound that BP would go out of business and that Libya would take them over!

Remember, it is vital to have a contrarian mindset if you want to make money in the financial markets, even though it goes against your natural instincts! In fact, if your decision is against your natural instincts you will probably make a very good trading or investment decision!

Finally, (just to hammer home the point) remember the financial crisis of 2008 when Lehman Brothers went out of business in late September. Also, during December 2008 and January 2009, the banking sector (we were told) was in shambles and the US Government (as it was reported) was going to have to take over Goldman Sachs. (Although now I think it is probably the other way around!)

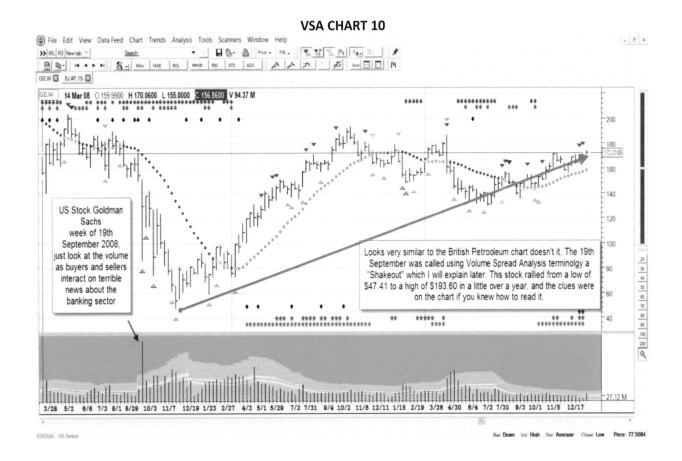

Let's look at the weekly chart, **VSA CHART 10**, and examine the Volume and what actually happened to the Goldman Sachs share price. Let's see if the Smart Money sent us a telegram then as they did with British Petroleum (BP).

We can see that just like BP the accumulation took place on bad news. After testing for supply in December 2008 and January 2009, the stock took off because demand had overcome supply.

If you had switched on your TV, or read the newspapers during December 2008 and January 2009, you would have been forgiven for thinking that the banks were finished and the TARP money meant the government would be in control making the banks shares worthless.

Of course that never happened and some of the biggest bonuses ever paid were given out to the bankers in 2010, only two years after the crisis began. In the 1960's, Richard Ney's number plate of his Rolls Royce read 'Wake Up!', and if you take on board his subliminal message you will make money in the financial markets.

CHAPTER 5
How to Read Charts like a Professional Trader

When a trader or investor looks at a price chart of a particular instrument, they may not be aware of how valuable the information contained within the chart can be. Learning to read a price chart is like learning to read sheet music in order to play a musical instrument. With the right instruction, practice, patience, and perseverance it is possible for virtually anyone to play a musical instrument.

I remember taking piano lessons when I was eight years old. I did not enjoy learning to play the piano because I lacked in the three 'P's which are practice, patience, and perseverance. Luckily, my teacher was very good. After three months I could read basic music and actually play a tune. Trading and investing is very similar, although there is a fourth 'P' that you must have and that fourth 'P' stands for plan.

You must develop a Volume Spread Analysis trading plan.

I truly believe that the majority of retail traders and investors of all experience levels can be successful and profitable in the financial markets if they are given the right instruction, then just apply the four 'P's to refine and develop those skills. In my travels, I have met thousands of traders and investors from all over the world. I quickly discovered that the top traders and consistently profitable fund managers all had certain important qualities in common. The vast majority was able to read a chart and used Volume Analysis as a key part of their trading and investment evaluation and they all understood 'the game' we are in and they knew how to win it!

Timing is also a key part of investing, especially in the stock market. As I write this book during 2010 and 2011, many retail traders and investors have fled the stock market only to watch it rally from the March 2010 low to then make new two-year highs during February 2011.

As the great investor Warren Buffet so wisely pointed out, "Most people get interested in stocks when everyone else is. The time to get interested is when *no one* else is. You can't buy what is popular and do well."

The British Petroleum stock price nearly doubling during the oil spill crisis really proves Buffet's quote to be true. In January 2011, we were seeing many investors and traders run to gold, silver, and bonds. I received an email from a long-standing customer of TradeGuider Systems, which was entitled *"Gold, Stocks and the Dollar: The Rise and Fall of a Correlation"* written by Peter Cohan on AOL Daily Finance, January 24th 2011.

In the article, Mr. Cohan describes the trend of ATM machines that deal in gold bullion beginning to dot the landscape of the USA, a trend that had also happened in Germany, amongst other places. On December 2nd, 2010 I posted a video on YouTube (see the TradeGuider channel) and warned that there was a bubble forming, impending the fall of silver. Ironically, all the analysts were also bullish just as they were when they predicted oil going to $200 a barrel in 2008, as we have already seen. The silver futures fell from the January 3rd high of $30.440 in the SLV futures, down to a January 26th 2011 low of $26.30.

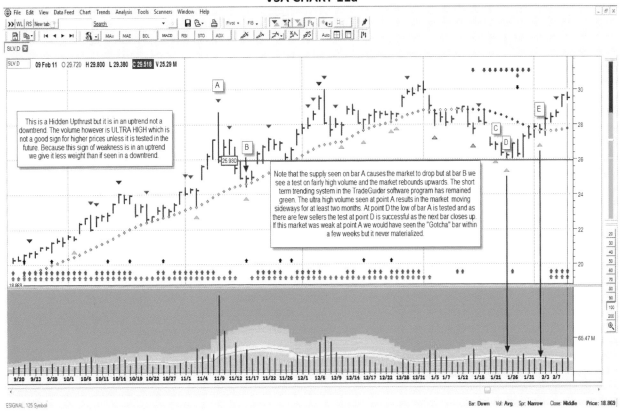

When we look closely at the chart, a number of important points are in evidence. We can see at point A on **VSA CHART 11a** that on November 9th, 2010 we see ultra high Volume. The TradeGuider software detects this and has placed a red indicator above the bar. This shows a *Sign of Weakness* called a *Hidden Up-thrust* determined by the Volume Spread Analysis methodology. In the TradeGuider software, all the indicators have numbers and dialogue boxes that explain the condition that has triggered the indicator with a description of what to look out for in the future. (You can find a glossary of indicators by number, as well their description in Volume 2 of the book, *"VSA Trade Sequences Explained".*)

Notice that the market tests the price level at point B and never begins to trend down, so this is a clear sign that higher prices are still likely, so do not short here.

It is very important to note that just because an indicator is red, it doesn't mean take a short position immediately and it is the same when a green indicator appears, it doesn't mean take a long position immediately. The Volume Spread Analysis methodology was developed to find imbalances in the supply/demand situation on any chart and in any time frame since these imbalances are happening every second the market is traded. In fact, they are happening tick by tick, which is why Tick Volume is extremely powerful to evaluate when used in the Volume Spread Analysis methodology, as we shall see later.

Volume Spread Analysis looks at three vital criteria to determine if a market is strong or weak. In a strong market, we look for opportunities to buy or go long. In a weak market, we look for opportunities to sell or to go short. We will identify specific Volume Spread Analysis trade set-ups later in this book.

The criteria that are used to identify imbalances in the supply and demand situation are based on the three Universal Laws that control the markets. Just like the Law of Gravity explains how human beings do not float off into space, the following three laws when understood on the price chart make the difference between a gambler and a professional profitable trader/investor. **The Universal Laws governing all market behavior are**:

- The Law of Supply and Demand

- The Law of Cause and Effect

- The Law of Effort versus Result (there is one other Universal law that does not relate to the charts, but I will cover that in Chapter 9)

So, Volume Spread Analysis looks at the following three criteria to determine supply and demand imbalances:

- **Volume** (most often displayed at the bottom of the chart and available in most good charting software)

- **Price Spread or range of price bar** (the high and low of the price bar in any time frame)

- **Closing Price on the bar** (Volume Spread Analysis does not use the open of the bar because it does not show us the result of the activity on the bar)

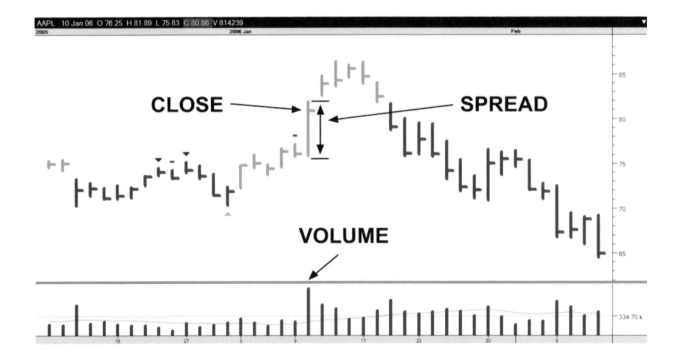

Supply and Demand, Cause and Effect, and Effort vs. Result can be observed in the action on price and amount of market movement in any given time frame.

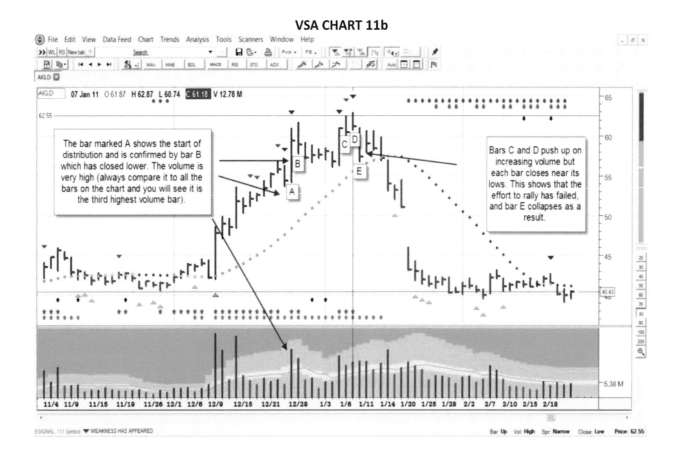

VSA CHART 11b

In **VSA CHART 11b**, which is the US stock AIG, we can see ultra high Volume coming in on the daily chart at point A, which is an up bar. An up bar is a price bar that has closed higher than the close of the preceding bar with a wide Spread price bar that closes off the high of the bar (about 20% off the high). If we were observing an effort for the price to rise on that Volume only to then see that the very next bar, bar B has closed lower, we can see that there must be selling in the ultra high Volume.

It is an early warning that distribution (selling) is beginning from one or more professional or institutional groups. This is not a place to short.

Even though we have an early warning sign that distribution is taking place, we are still in an up-trend and we want to find the highest probability trades. **For shorting the market, opportunities appear in down-trends.**

At point C and D we see the stock attempt to go up. Volume on D is higher than C, but as a typical telltale sign, at the end of each bar, the price closes at, or near, the low of the price bar. This is *No Result from an Effort to Rally* and can also be called an *Up-thrust*, which is a stop hunting move by the professionals.

Both *No Result from Effort* and *Up-thrusts* are very similar in nature and it is most important to keep in mind the following:

- **If in an up-trend, do not short an *Up-thrust* or *No Result from Effort* if you have strength (buying) in the background** (like the BP example).

- **Always look for shorts when we have weakness in the background** (like the JP Morgan example). When we see these indications in a bull market, it simply means that the market is not ready to move up just at that moment and you will often see the market rest or fall a little before the rally resumes if it is in a bull-run (technical analysts call this a 1-2-3 pattern. Another way to understand the price action dynamics is to think of climbing a mountain. The path to the top is usually a series of peaks and valleys, which the chartist calls **retracements**).

- **If in a down-trending market with a serious *Sign of Weakness* in the background, it is a very powerful sell opportunity!** We would look to go short (or for selling opportunities) as the market rises (retraces).

- If using a trend channel, we would look to sell the retracement at the top of the down-trend channel using a VSA principle showing selling or lack of buying/demand from the Smart Money.

Up-trends

Always remember that we look to go long (buying opportunities) as the market falls using a VSA principle showing buying or lack of selling by the professionals (if using a trend channel, look at the bottom of the channel).

Down-trends

We look to go short (selling opportunities) as the market rises, using a VSA principle that shows selling or lack of buying (demand) from the professionals (if using a trend channel, look at the top of the channel).

As we have already mentioned, **weakness appears on an up bar and strength appears on a down bar.** It makes perfect sense when you consider that the Smart Money will want to sell at higher prices than their purchase price and buy at lower prices to in order to make a profit when they sell. "Buy low, sell high" is the old adage and it is evident in the chart when you can read it.

SCHEMATIC EXAMPLE
Overbought/oversold areas in a trend does not matter whether it is up or down

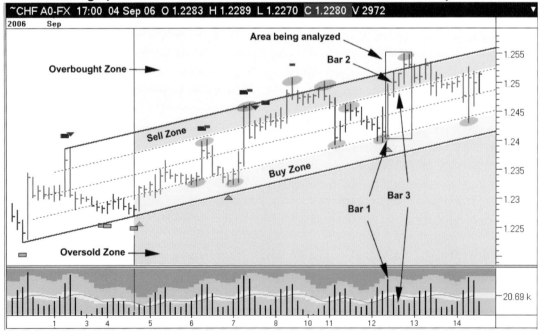

Trend Channels and Trigger Numbers

For example, in an *up-trend*, the use of a trend channel is very important to identify if you are in an overbought or oversold area of the trend. If you are long and enter an overbought area of a trend channel, you are vulnerable to profit taking from professional groups. This profit taking will result in a fall of prices back into the channel as shown in bars 1, 2, and 3 in the Schematic. It is the opposite if you are short and in a *down-trend* and you enter an oversold area of a trend channel (which is the lower trend line of the channel).

Drawing a Trend Channel to Identify Your Current Trading Zone

When Tom Williams was asked to join the trading syndicate in Beverly Hills, his main job was to construct the charts that the syndicate would use to analyze to make their trading decisions.

Since there were no computers in those days, Tom would use a 5-foot ruler (which he still has today) and have the chart laid out on a 9-foot table. One of the most important parts of Tom's chart drafting responsibility was to draw trend channels on the charts. Drawing a trend channel allows the trader or investor to see buying or selling opportunities as a market approaches either the top or bottom of the channel. When drawing a Wyckoff Trend Channel, Tom followed some simple rules:

- **Choose your time frames.** For example, if trading stocks and are holding medium to long term (3 months to 3 years or more) select three time frames, such as monthly, weekly, and daily. Start with the biggest time frame first, which is the monthly in this case, and put up 120 bars or 10 years of data (markets work in cycles and the 10 year cycle is widely recognized as a major cycle).

- **If trading intraday, choose time frames that work for your trading style.** So if scalping the E-mini S&P for 8 ticks, you will look at a 15 minute, a 5 minute and a 3 minute time frame.

- **If trading forex (currencies) and have a buy and hold strategy for hours or days, there is no right or wrong time frame so you may want to sample different time frames.** You may want to try a 4 hour, 1 hour, and a 15 minute chart. I have found that my best time frames have come from trial and error. Now take the largest time frame chart first and put up at least 750 price bars (the TradeGuider software allows 2000 bars if the data is available).

In **VSA CHART 12** we will examine the continuous contract of the CME Group currency futures 6B #F, which is the futures contract of the US dollar versus UK pound. I have used a 240 minute time frame, which means that each price bar is formed every four hours. This chart gives us a clear view of the bigger picture and we then can look for the last active trend, which in this case is an up-trend that commenced in early January.

At point A on **VSA CHART 12**, we note the ultra high Volume and start our trend channel by selecting the bottom of the bar at point A because we have made at least two higher lows previously. At point B, we again note the ultra high Volume since the market pulls back and select point B as our second low. The reason why we select B and not the other two pullbacks in this up-trend is because point B shows the highest Volume.

TradeGuider software automatically selected point C because it is the intersecting high. The channel is now projected out and will remain on the chart until it is deleted or modified.

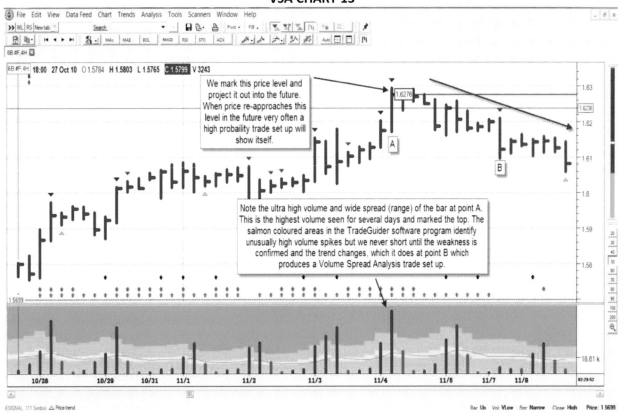

We note on **VSA CHART 13** that the market hits serious resistance on November 4th 2010 and we see an ultra high Volume up bar with a wide Spread that actually reverses the trend and results in a 949 tick down move. That price level will become a Volume Spread Analysis *Trigger Number* in the future as price re-approaches that level. It will give an excellent Volume Spread Analysis trade set-up.

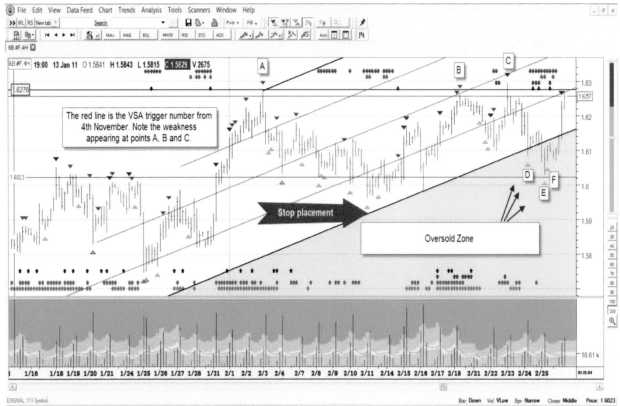

VSA CHART 14 shows the best place to buy an instrument that is in the oversold zone of an up-trend when a strong VSA principle appears. In this case we have a cluster of green indicators shown at D, E, and F. The first of the three green indicators is called ***Stopping Volume***. This indicator is often seen in an up-trend as professionals mark the price down for more buying. If you had gone long at point D, you would not be in the oversold zone and would be under pressure as the price is marked down for more buying at point E, a *Shakeout*.

A *Shakeout* is a much stronger indication of strength because we are into the oversold zone. Bar E has ultra high Volume but closes in the middle of the bar, showing that buying must be taking place causing it to close in the middle. But what makes this set-up more powerful is what happens on bar F, which is the right next to bar E and has the last green indicator present. This is called a ***Two Bar Reversal.***

When a *Two Bar Reversal* is seen after a *Shakeout*, it will be extremely bullish. The market retraces two bars after the reversal, but the Volume on these bars is extremely low showing that there is no professional activity as the price falls. This is confirms the bullish bars at E and F. This is a strong buy indication seen at the bottom of an up-trend channel.

It is highly recommended that the stop should be placed at the last point of accumulation (buying), which is at or near the bottom of the up-trend channel and is marked with a red arrow on **VSA CHART 14** and preferably on an odd number.

Stop placement varies from market to market and also depends on risk/reward ratios, loss tolerance, account size, and individual trading style. As a general rule, if I trade using a wider stop, I start by placing less contracts and then scale into the position as the trade moves in my favor.

When trading currencies or forex, a wider stop is often required especially when news events trigger massive moves. I try to avoid being in the currency market if a major news announcement is coming, such as FOMC meeting minutes or unemployment numbers. I like to trade the reaction after the news is released. You will often find the market is marked up on the news to encourage traders to go long if the news is bullish, only to find that the market quickly turns against them as selling takes place into the surge of buying.

Going Long at Support in an Up-trend

When we use Volume Spread Analysis techniques to identify trade set-ups, we are looking for the highest probability of success. If you go long at the bottom of an up-trend channel when the market is in a clear up-trend gives you a higher probability of success.

Going Short at Resistance in an Down-trend

The same goes for going short at the top of a down-trend channel when the market is in a clear down-trend and a clear Volume Spread Analysis principle appears.

If you jumped into a fast flowing river and attempted to swim against the current, you would use a lot of effort and you may make little or no progress if the current is forceful. This is similar to going short against an up-trend or going long against a down-trend.

However, when a VSA trigger number is hit, there is opportunity to make money trading against the bigger trend (i.e. countertrend). Using the same example, the 6B #F currency futures contract, let us examine a set-up to the short side against the bigger trend and we will analyze two other time frames to identify a good entry.

Multiple Time Frame Considerations

When going short against the trend, there are five important questions you should be able to answer "Yes" to:

- Are you at a VSA trigger number showing resistance to higher prices?

- Are you at the top of one of the quadrants of the up-trend channel in the biggest time frame, or even better, are you in an overbought zone?

The quadrants are the 4 lines that break the trend channel into 4 parts as shown in **VSA CHART 14**. Point B is clearly right on the top of the center quadrant and Point C is approaching the center quadrant, but both points would attract interest because of the resistance seen at Point A. Ask yourself:

- Is there a clear VSA (Volume Spread Analysis) principle present?

- Is the market beginning to mushroom over, or top out and begin a down-trend in the smaller time frames?

- Do you have any strength or obvious buying indications in the near background on the largest time frame?

We have seen in **VSA CHART 14** that resistance to higher prices is seen at points A, B, and C at around the 1.6275 price area. When price re-approaches this area at 1.6275 we look for *Signs of Weakness* to appear when professionals try to catch the breakout traders.

This is very profitable for the professionals because most uninformed traders see the high Volume coming in and the price spiking through resistance. Most often and incorrectly, the uninformed traders believe that the high Volume must be buying causing the price to rise.

However, as we have already demonstrated, professionals often take the opportunity to sell into the rising prices. We see the result of this selling as the price falls back into the channel at points A, B and C on **VSA CHART 14**. Now we must go down one or two time frames to look for our optimum entry. In this case, we will examine the sell (shorting) opportunity shown at point B on **VSA CHART 14**.

Having seen the weakness appearing on the larger time frame, we drop down to the 4 hour chart, the 1 hour chart, and lastly the 15 minute chart, as shown in **VSA CHARTS 15** and **16**.

VSA CHART 15

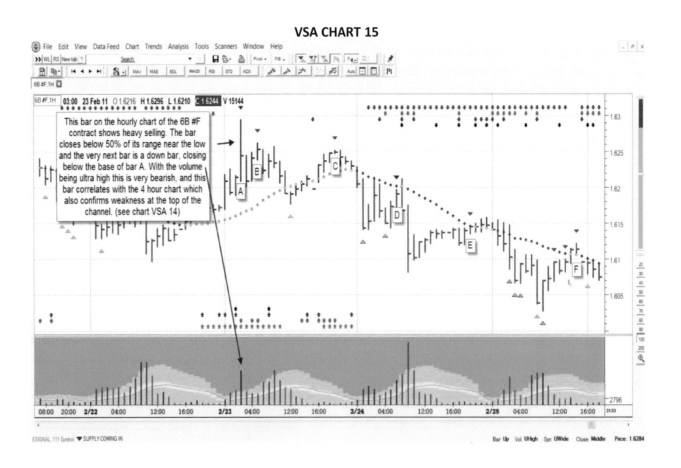

VSA CHART 15 shows the hourly chart of the 6B #F contract, the same chart we saw in **VSA CHART 14,** but this time we have moved down a time frame.

At Point A, we see an ultra high Volume bar that has a very wide Spread, but closes below the middle of the bar. The very next bar confirms the weakness as it closes below the base of bar A. There must have been selling into bar A, the start of distribution by professionals.

At Point B, we now have a Volume Spread Analysis signal called *No Demand after Serious Weakness.* Look at Point B and closely examine the Volume and the price bar.

We note bar B attempts to go up into the body of bar A where the ultra high Volume has been seen, but at bar B, we note that the Volume is declining and is very low. Bar B is an up bar, a price bar that closes higher than the bar behind it and the Volume on bar B is less than the previous two bars. We have declining Volume on what is an up bar. The Spread of the bar is very narrow, especially when compared with bar A.

We should consider what's going on here because the professionals have sold into bar A at the top of the larger time frame trend channel at resistance. As the market goes back up at bar B, professionals withdraw their interest in higher prices because they have already sold at bar A and they now know the market is a weak market. The Volume on bar B confirms their lack of interest because it is now low.

Could we take a short at point B or C?

Well, it is more risky than at points D, E, and F and that is because the market is still in an up-trend on all the time frames from the 4 hour time frame down to the 15 minute time frame. When I take a trade, I grade the trade from 1 to 3.

Grade 1 is a high probability trade with Grade 3 being more risky. If a short position was taken at point B or C, I would grade it a 3, but a short taken at D, E, and F would be a Grade 2 because the trend is moving into a short-term down-trend on two of the three time frames. Why would I not grade it a 1, you may ask?

It is simply because the predominant trend is an up-trend and I am therefore counter-trend trading the larger time frame. Grade 1 trades happen when all the trends align in your chosen time frames and a Volume Spread Analysis principle appears.

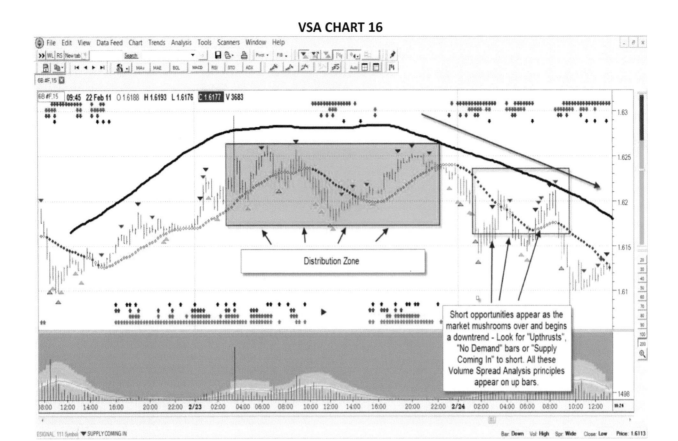

Let's look at the same information in a 15 minute time frame on **VSA CHART 16**.

We are looking for evidence that the market is mushrooming over at the top. Only one thing causes the mushrooming over and that is professional selling or distribution. It will always appear first on the smallest time frame you are using and then become apparent on the larger time frame, which is why it is important to analyze multiple time frames.

After a serious *Sign of Weakness* appears, which in the 6B #F example was evident in all three time frames chosen for analysis, look for the characteristic mushroom-top price pattern that will begin to form on the lower time frame. This is called the **distribution zone** and is where the professionals are selling or withdrawing their interest in higher prices.

If we see distribution happening and the market is in a down-trend, this will offer great opportunities to short. If we see accumulation happening and the market is in an up-trend, then this will offer great opportunities to go long.

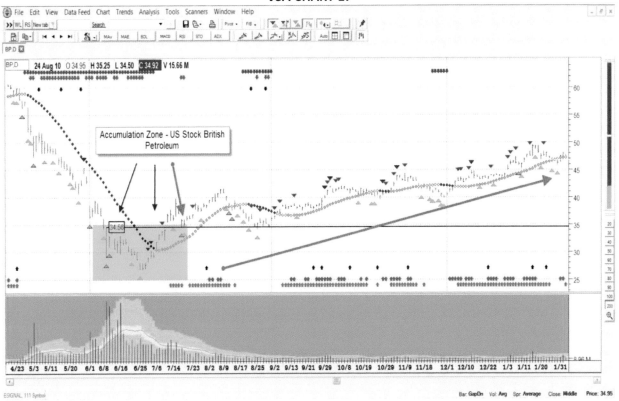

VSA CHART 17 shows the accumulation zone on US stock chart of British Petroleum (BP). After we see accumulation, we look for Volume Spread Analysis indicators of strength such as *Stopping Volume*, *No Supply,* and a *Test in a Rising Market*. Note the ultra high Volume on the down bar as accumulation begins.

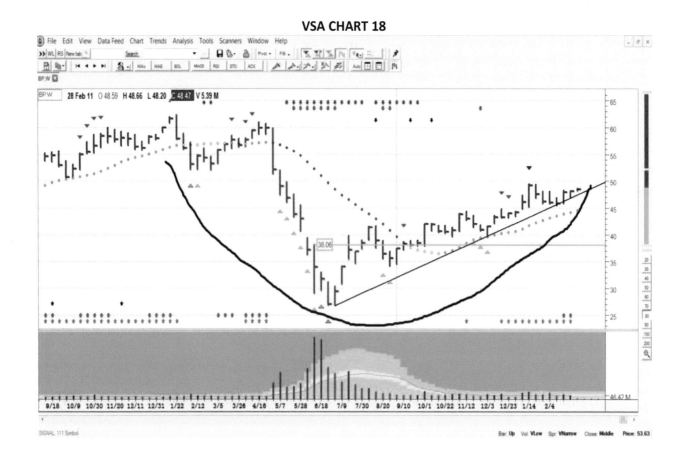

On **VSA CHART 18** (the weekly chart of British Petroleum), we see the opposite of the mushrooming over when we see distribution. We now have a saucer-shape forming at the bottom as the price begins to rally after accumulation has been successful.

CHAPTER 6
Key Principles of the Volume Spread Analysis Methodology
Part 1: Weakness

In Chapter 5, I introduced some terms used in the Volume Spread Analysis methodology. In this chapter, we'll discuss the definition of each of the terms, as well as their meaning on a chart. As per previous chapters of this book, I will continue the convention of referring to Volume Spread Analysis as VSA, which is how it is often referred to in many trading rooms and forums. VSA is based around the analysis of the imbalances of supply and demand, which when they happen, provide trade set-ups to both the long and short side of the market.

VSA will identify *Signs of Strength and Signs of Weakness* in the markets. The TradeGuider software and Add-on Studies for other trading software programs produces indicators that are categorized as either *Signs of Strength*- colored in green with an indicator number beginning with *SOS* and *Signs of Weakness*- colored in red with an indicator number beginning with *SOW*.

As opposed to being buy or sell signals, these indicators measure imbalances of supply and demand. Although, when certain indicators appear, they can be considered very high probability market turning points, especially when confirmed by a secondary indicator when price action reacts at, or near, the area where the initial indicator appeared.

The Up-thrust

We'll first examine the key *Signs of Weakness* identified using VSA. **It is important to keep in mind that all principles can appear on your charts in different intensities.**

Also note that the principles of VSA work in all time frames. Whether you are scalping the market for a few ticks or investing long term in the stock market holding your positions for months, these principles can be used and adapted to your individual trading style and strategy.

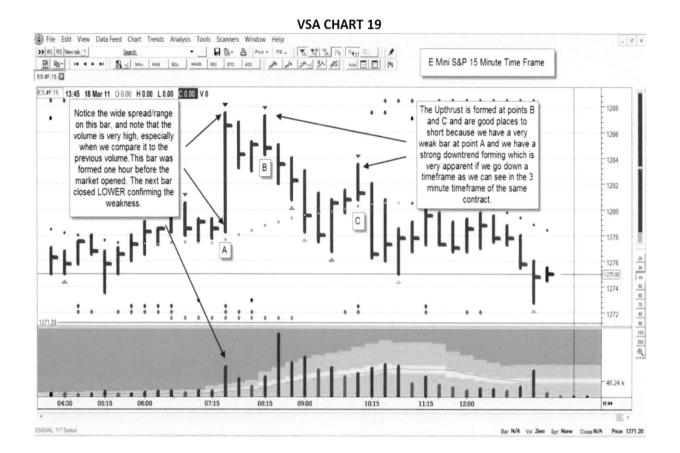

For an example we'll analyze two charts showing the same principle and how it moved the market. The first chart is a 15 minute E-mini S&P futures chart, **VSA CHART 19**. This chart shows two classic *Up-thrusts* resulting in a fall in price. In fact, it is a nine-point fall from where the first *Up-thrust* appeared at point B.

At point A, we have seen a very wide Spread on the bar and the Volume is ultra high when compared with the previous bars.

I have been asked a few times, "Does the spike in Volume we see when the markets open get incorrectly analyzed by the TradeGuider software?"

The answer is "No."

The spike in Volume is present because the Smart Money players are actively trading as the market opens. In the spot forex markets, this is usually due to the fact that the banks trade amongst themselves over the weekend and the retail market is not privy to this currency pricing until the markets re-open after the weekend.

The TradeGuider software will measure the Volume correctly because the information is coming from the exchange via the data feed provider. If the Volume is very high and is on an up bar, then this will produce a *Sign of Weakness*. As Tom showed me, markets do not like excessively high Volume on up bars. When you review your charts you will see that is often the case in the vast majority of charts you look at.

The only occasion where the market will not react negatively after ultra high Volume on an up bar is present is if the Smart Money is bullish and wants higher prices. In that case, you will see a *Sign of Strength* called a *Test* or *No-Supply* (there will be more about that in the section on *Signs of Strength*). We see at point A an extremely wide Spread bar on ultra high Volume and the closing price on the bar is near the top of the bar.

If this ultra high Volume had been more buying than selling, then surely the next bar would close higher, but it doesn't, as you can see. It closes nearly half way down the bar at point A and therefore must be considered a serious *Sign of Weakness*. With this weakness now apparent, we are looking for **confirmation** of that weakness to take a trade to the short side of the market (sell).

Could you short the market at point A? Yes, some of our customers do take that trade, but I personally do not (although, Tom Williams would most likely also take the trade at that point).

The reason I do not take the short trade at point A is because we still have a strong up-trend in place on all time frames and I want to 'go with the flow'. This means I always seek to trade in harmony with the trend.

If I am going to go swimming in the Chicago River (which I have never done), I know it has a strong current, so I would make far more progress trying to swim *with* the current, as opposed to against the current. This is much like taking a short trade in a rising market. You can certainly make winning trades shorting in a rising market, especially if price action gets to the top of the up-trend channel when the market is vulnerable to the Smart Money profit taking.

In my day trading I like to use at least three time frames to confirm the market is trending one way or the other and the TradeGuider software and add-in studies have two extremely valuable proprietary trending systems.

The Medium Term Trending System

The first trending system is called the **Medium Term Trending System** and colors the bars blue for an up-trend and red for a down-trend (colors are customizable).

The Diamond Trending System

The second trending system is called the **Diamond Trending System** and can produce a green, white, or red diamond on or near the price bar. This is a short-term trending system and is very good for scalping. The green diamonds show an up-trend, the red diamonds show a down-trend, and the white diamonds show a potential change of trend coming.

You can see these clearly in **VSA CHART 20**. **VSA CHART 20** is the 3 minute time frame of the E-mini S&P of the same information shown in **VSA CHART 19** (15 minute chart).

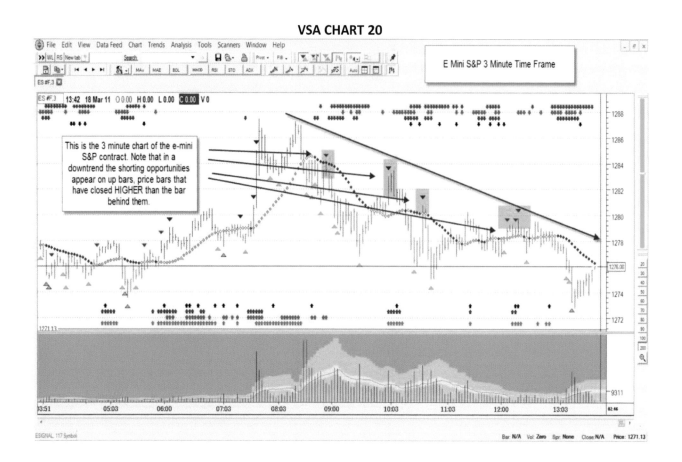

The *Up-thrust* can appear on ultra high Volume, high Volume, average Volume and low Volume. The purpose of the *Up-thrust* is to catch stops of those that are short in a weak market, encourage buyers who see the price rising quickly and rush to get in. Often, the *Up-thrust* catches breakout traders because they often happen at pivot points or resistance levels.

The *Up-thrust* that has the highest probability of making you money will appear with the following rules, which should always be remembered:

- Before the *Up-thrust* has appeared you should see in the background a serious *Sign of Weakness*, such as a *Buying Climax, Supply Overcoming Demand, Supply Coming In,* or the *End of a Rising Market* (which I will show you). This will usually be apparent by looking back at 50 price bars.

- The market you are trading should be in a down-trend in at least 3 time frames.

- Price action should be at, or near the top of the down-trend channel in 2 time frames.

- If using the TradeGuider system you should have at least 5 red diamonds on the shortest time frame you are using, this is showing a short-term down-trend.

- If using the TradeGuider system you should have at least 3 red price bars on at least three time frames, this is showing a medium term down-trend.

The highest probability trade set-up to the short side is when you see an ultra high Volume *Up-thrust* after you have seen a serious *Sign of Weakness* such as a *Buying Climax*. The *Up-thrusts* shown in **VSA CHART 19** are appearing on high Volume, not ultra high Volume. If these *Up-thrusts* were observed on ultra high Volume, the likelihood of a bigger downward move on price is greatly increased. When I describe a Volume bar as being climactic, it simply means that the Smart Money and the Herd are all involved causing massive Volume, which is identified by the TradeGuider program as ultra high Volume.

When ultra high Volume is seen on your charts it often marks the reversal point of a trend, or a pull-back in the trend. This is why you should pay very close attention when you see ultra high Volume appearing because an opportunity to make money is presenting itself. The Smart Money leave footprints on your charts and the ability to recognize these footprints are the key to being a consistent winner.

At point B on **VSA CHART 19** we have what is called a *Hidden Up-thrust*. It is considered hidden because if we examine the *Up-thrust* at point C, we can see that the entire *Up-thrust* bar is formed above the close of the previous bar. The *Up-thrust* formed at point B has closed below the close of the previous bar, as well as in the body of the previous bar and is therefore called a *Hidden Up-thrust*. Both of these *Up-thrusts* are in the right place.

When I say "in the right place", I'm referring to a rising market where you have *Signs of Strength* in the background, which you will often see what looks like an *Up-thrust* appearing. The individual bars will look similar to the bars at point B and C on **VSA CHART 19**. However, if there are *Signs of Strength,* or climactic buying signs have appeared and the market is going up, then the *Up-thrust* is in the wrong place. **To take a short trade when an *Up-thrust* appears you must see climactic selling in the background, just like the example in VSA CHART 19.**

It is much like going to the Arctic and seeing a polar bear on the ice. The polar bear is in the right place. However, if you are sunbathing on a beach in Hawaii and a polar bear walks right by you, then that polar bear is definitely in the wrong place - you better hope it escaped from the zoo, or else you're just hallucinating!

Remember, looking for *Up-thrusts* is like looking for polar bears in the arctic. Look for *Up-thrusts* that have appeared **after** a serious *Sign of Weakness* for less risky trade should be in a down-trend.

The Buying Climax

A *Buying Climax* is an extremely powerful *Sign of Weakness* and will often mark the top of a market. When *a Buying Climax* is seen, it will come after a bull run has taken place, so it will appear in an up-trend. Whenever *Climactic Action* appears on your charts, it will appear on high or ultra high Volume (the higher the Volume, the better) and this will show that both the Smart Money *and* the uninformed Herd have become extremely active. The *Buying Climax* always appears on an up bar (a price bar that has closed higher than the preceding bar) with a wide Spread and Closing Price near the middle of the bar.

The **Buying Climax** occurs because after a period of rising prices in a bull market, the Herd is afraid they are going to miss out on the next move up. For the most part, some type of unusually great news about the instrument that is being traded will accompany this. In stocks, it will probably be a great earnings report, or some sort of rumor about a buy out or merger. As the price rallies, the Smart Money sell into the rush of buy orders coming in and due to the feverish activity, the Spread of the bar widens.

Only one thing can cause the price to close in the middle of the bar when the Volume is ultra high, which is sell orders satisfying the Herd's buy orders from the Smart Money. After you see this *Sign of Weakness*, you will often see the market move sideways for 10 or 20 bars with additional *Signs of Weakness* appearing afterwards. The most common *SOW* is a *No Demand* signal, which we'll look at next. After I see a *Buying Climax*, I wait for the market to penetrate the low of that *Buying Climax* bar.

This can happen within 25 bars, but note that sometimes the market can turn quickly in under 25 bars, but at other times it can take longer.

There is no exact science here. You must read the charts and watch the bars as they form and wait for the trend of price to move down away from the low of the *Buying Climax* bar. Once the market turns down and begins to form a down-trend, we can now look for *Up-thrusts* and *No-Demand* bars, or *Supply Coming In.*

Remember, selling happens on up bars and so does lack of demand. When you see high or ultra high Volume on up bars, the Smart Money players are actively selling which is the cause of the high/ultra high Volume. If you see low Volume up bars in the same price area where you observed the high/ultra high Volume, this **confirms** the weakness. This is because the low Volume on the up bars show that the Smart Money are withdrawing their interest in higher prices. They are not active, which can be seen on the chart by the low Volume on the up bars.

Low Volume represents low activity and it is the activity of the Smart Money we are interested in. If they are not interested in higher prices, then you shouldn't be, either.

They are not interested because they have seen the *Buying Climax* in the background.

Buying Climaxes appear in all markets and in all time frames. If you observe a *Buying Climax* on a 1 minute futures chart, the resultant move will be a lot less in terms of points, versus you observing a *Buying Climax* on a weekly chart of the same instrument. The effect will be the same. The market will fall because selling has taken place in the *Buying Climax* bar.

Since all markets work on the law of supply and demand, the VSA principles in this book will apply in any time frame- even on tick charts. Whether you are scalping the market or holding longer-term investment portfolios, Volume Spread Analysis can be applied to your style of trading and chart analysis.

Wyckoff discussed the market moving in phases. If you observe the charts closely, you will see he was absolutely correct. Knowing which phase of the market you are trading in is so important that I must dedicate a whole chapter to this very subject!

When a *Buying Climax* is observed, it is known as the beginning of the distribution phase. In order to distribute, the Herd need to be buying at the new highs that are being created.

A genuine *Buying Climax,* as described by Wyckoff, should be into fresh new ground, meaning that there is no price action in that same area for at least 500 bars or more in any time frame. In Volume Spread Analysis we often see *Buying Climaxes* being identified by the TradeGuider computer program even though the *Buying Climax* has appeared within 500 bars of price action. These should not be ignored because they are still considered a powerful *Sign of Weakness.*

As with many Volume Spread Analysis trade set-ups, we must wait for confirmation before jumping in to the trade. This requires patience. After a *Buying Climax* has been observed, the market may go up further, even though selling has begun by the Smart Money. This is due to momentum.

To give you an example of **momentum**, imagine a car is driving up a steep hill and the driver has his foot flat down on the gas pedal. The car will gain speed slowly until it meets the limit of the engine's capacity to go faster. So, if the driver removes his foot from the pedal does the car coast to a halt instantly? Of course not! Momentum carries the car further forward!

If the brakes aren't applied and no gas is pumped into the engine, the car will naturally be propelled further up the hill by the momentum that was generated by the earlier application of gas. The car will eventually slow down to a crawl and then stop. This this is exactly what I want you to see happening on a chart. The market simply runs out of energy to go further and it coasts slowly to a stop at new highs.

VSA CHART 21

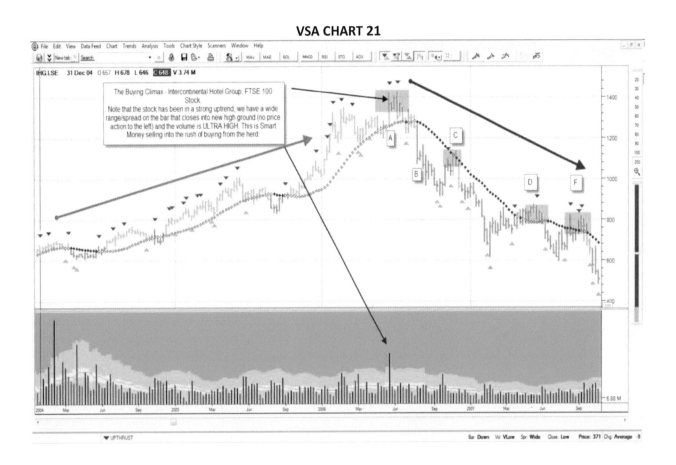

At this point, the market doesn't suddenly collapse, but you will often see the market move sideways for a few bars with narrowing Spreads on the bars. Then, as the down-trend begins, you will observe additional phases of distribution.

Remember, these phases will appear on up bars as the market is trying to rally in a down-trend. This can be seen clearly in **VSA CHART 21**, a weekly chart of a UK stock. Note that after the *Buying Climax* at point A, the stock takes two months to begin the decline. Shorting opportunities, or places to buy puts, are evident at points C, D, and E (puts are for those who are options traders). We see examples of *Up-thrusts, No Demand*, and *Supply Coming In*, all of which are identified by proprietary indicators in the TradeGuider software.

Note that the bar at point B is extremely important because it is confirming the weakness. At point B we have a down bar with average Volume, but the Spread is very wide. Most importantly, we see this bar after the *Buying Climax* and this wide Spread bar takes out all the price action that had been acting as prior support for the previous 7 months or so. This is a *Gotcha bar* and it imprisons weak holders who are stuck long in a bad trade.

If you see *No Demand* at this same level in the future, which we can clearly identify at point C on **VSA CHART 21** (where the red TradeGuider indicator is shown) and again highlighted by the two red arrows in **VSA CHART 22**, then this now becomes a high probability trade to short this stock.

Remember, this set-up can appear in all markets regardless of time frame, so study it carefully.

VSA CHART 22

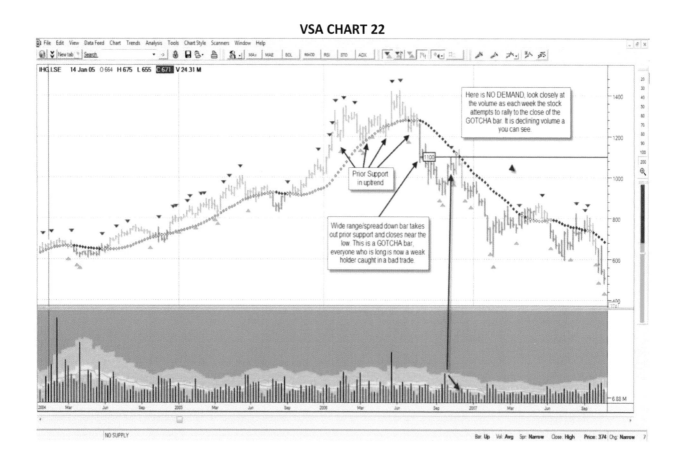

No Demand

There are 3 types of *No Demand* bars that will appear on a chart:

- *No Demand* in an up-trend

- *No Demand* in a down-trend

- *No Demand* at market tops

The best place to take a short when you see a *No Demand* bar is in a down-trend, especially after you have seen some sign of *Climactic Action,* such as what we just saw in the explanation of a *Buying Climax*. More aggressive traders who use Volume Spread Analysis, including Tom Williams, will immediately short a *No Demand* bar if it comes after a serious *Sign of Weakness,* such as the *Buying Climax* or the *End of a Rising Market* (which we will look at next because it is my favorite indicator to go short on).

No Demand has a good probability of being a good short trade especially if it is at the same price level of the climactic bar. Why? The market will not rally and breach the climactic bar on very low Volume.

So what exactly does *No Demand* mean from a Volume Spread Analysis perspective?

It simply means that there is no interest in higher prices from the Smart Money in the time frame in which you see the indicator appear. Like many TradeGuider indicators, *No Demand* requires confirmation. *No Demand* can be confirmed when the next bar closes lower than the *No Demand* bar. However, this is where many of new traders learning Volume Spread Analysis get confused. As I have already mentioned, *No Demand* bars come in three types:

- *No Demand* in an up-trend

- *No Demand* in a down-trend

- *No Demand* at market tops

Following is **VSA CHART 23** which shows an example of *No Demand* in an up-trend.

I highly recommend you do not try to take shorts when you see *No Demand* in an up-trend because although the indicator will often cause the market to go down a few bars, it can quickly rebound upwards due to the trend of price. The up-trend will have been the result of some climactic action on down bars in the background and it will make the market a strong market, not a weak one. Let's review:

- ***Climactic Buying*** is the Smart Money selling to the rush of buying from the Herd. This usually happens at market tops***. Bearish!***

- ***Climactic Selling*** is Smart Money buying from the rush of selling from the Herd. This happens at market bottoms, often accompanied by very bad news. ***Bullish!***

No Demand in an Up-trend, Not Bearish

In **VSA CHART 23** we can see a clear example of *No Demand* in an up-trend after climactic buying has taken place. This is an hour chart of the E-mini S&P futures continuous contract. At point A, we see a wide Spread down bar appear. The market fell from the prior day's high and the market opened trying to move lower than the previous day's close. Ultra high Volume is seen at bar A, which is often evident when the major markets open around the world, simply because that is when the Smart Money usually becomes extremely active.

When the market goes lower than the previous day's close and the Volume is ultra high, many breakout traders go short, wrongly thinking that this feverish activity on a down bar is selling. At bar B, it confirms there must be more buying in bar A because it rallies away and closes above the entire Spread of bar A.

This is called a *Two Bar Reversal*.

The result of these two bars is that the market becomes a strong market and begins to rally. At bar C, the TradeGuider software shows a red indicator. This is *No Demand in an Up-trend*. The up-trend is clearly identified in TradeGuider by the software's two proprietary trending systems that show green diamonds and blue bars. The *No Demand* indicator has the following characteristics:

- *No Demand* is seen on an up bar, which is a price bar that closes higher than the bar(s) behind it.

- The Spread of the bar is narrow.

- The Closing Price should be on the high of the bar, but we do see *No Demand* bars that close in the middle or on the low. The principle of *No Demand* in an up-trend is still valid as the long as the close of the current bar is higher than the close of the previous bar.

- The Volume will be less than the previous two bars.

At point C on **VSA CHART 23**, the TradeGuider software causes a VSA indicator to appear. It is colored red and it is called *No Demand.*

As you learn Volume Spread Analysis, you will observe that just 4 bars back were two very strong *Signs of Strength* on high Volume. If you have the TradeGuider software, you will have a dialogue box that appears when you left-click on your mouse and it will explain the situation that the indicator should appear in. The text in this dialogue box will indicate that you should see weakness in the background, but in this example we have strength. We are starting an up-trend.

Also, to confirm a *No Demand* bar the next bar should be down, but the next bar closes up. It is not confirmed so therefore, we can ignore it (in other words, we have a polar bear in Hawaii – it is in the wrong place). If that indicator appeared in a down-trend after a *Buying Climax*, we would give that great attention and place a sell order below the bottom of the *No Demand* bar in order to let the market come to you. **You do not sell the market on *No Demand.***

Why? Because a *No Demand* bar will often be followed by an *Up-thrust*, which will put you under pressure or stop you out.

If you see a *No Demand* bar and then it is followed by an *Up-thrust*, move your sell order to below the bottom of the *Up-thrust*. Again, wait for the market to come to you just as you would have done with the *No Demand* set-up. **I cannot stress this enough- this should always be in a down-trend!**

At point D, we once again see an indicator that is identified as *No Demand* by the TradeGuider software and in this case the next bar closes lower. Note that the lower closing bar never takes out the bottom of bar D and this is again in a strong up-trend. Ignore it. ***No Demand* short trades are higher probability in down-trends.**

When I asked Tom why *No Demand* bars appear in up-trends, he said it was because the Smart Money have to buy on down bars at lower prices. So in an up move, they will withdraw interest at certain price levels because they want to buy at lower prices because they are bullish. That, of course, will result in low Volume on the up bars hence why you see the VSA *Sign of Weakness* in both up-trends and down-trends. **In up-trends, we want to pay close attention to *Signs of Strength*, not *Signs of Weakness*.** We want to trade in harmony with the Smart Money and not against it.

No Demand at Market Tops, Bearish

Earlier, we saw a very good example of *No Demand* at the top of the market on the weekly crude oil charts in 2008. However, really good and obvious opportunities come when we see *No Demand* after we have seen climactic action at market tops, such as the *Buying Climax* or *End of a Rising Market*.

No Demand that appears subsequently within 5 bars of a serious *Sign of Weakness* and into a new price action area (or at an old resistance level) is validly considered *No Demand*, thereby confirming the bearishness.

These set-ups will often appear when news is good and can sometimes come after a bar that has 'gapped up', which will excite the Herd to buy at these tops.

If you do decide that you are going to sell the market on the *No Demand* indication, beware of an *Up-thrust* and make sure there is a serious *Sign of Weakness* in the background (usually within 25 bars). If you see *Up-thrusts* after a serious *Sign of Weakness,* it means these *Up-thrusts* and *No Demand* bars are confirming the weakness.

I used to get stopped out by these *Up-thrusts* and Tom would encourage me to jump straight back into the market. He could now see the apparent weakness appearing on the chart. There were times, even in the early days, where I would hesitate only to watch the market plummet down after the *Up-thrust* had stopped me out.

I consider trading these *No Demand* set-ups at market tops to be aggressive trading, but if you have all the indicators showing weakness appearing at previous resistance levels, then the probability of the trade working is greatly increased.

VSA CHART 24

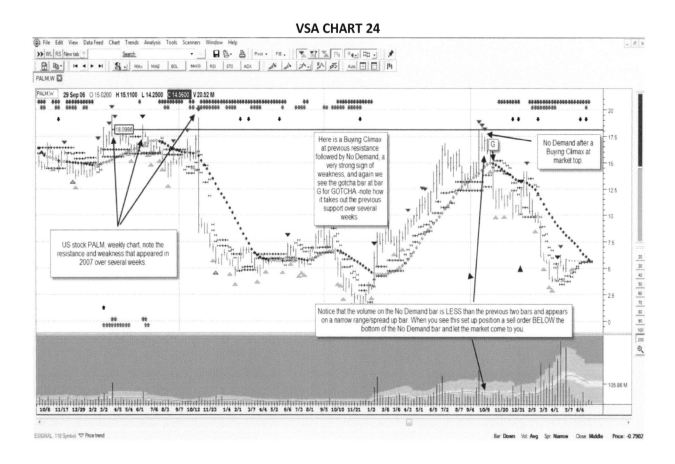

On **VSA CHART 24**, which is the weekly chart of US stock PALM, we observe the resistance to the left of the chart. This stock fails to penetrate the $17.50 level at least 4 times over several weeks during 2007. Finally, we see a collapse in price of nearly $100.00 on a wide Spread down bar closing near the low. At point G on **VSA CHART 24**, we see a very good example of a bar that locks you into a poor trade if you had gone long on the *Buying Climax* bar. Many traders and investors are now totally confused about what is going on.

The stock had been in a rally for many weeks prior to the *Buying Climax.* Two bars after the *Buying Climax* we see *No Demand.* Here, we see that *No Demand* is an up bar, which is a price bar that has closed higher than the previous bar, and the Volume (the activity) is now less than the previous two bars. It is in the right place due to the *Buying Climax* in immediate proximity (two bars prior).

The *No Demand* is caused by the lack of buying from the Smart Money because they sold two bars earlier. Evidently they are not interested in higher prices- the net result being that they withdraw their buying.

This causes the low Volume seen on the *No Demand* bar.

VSA CHART 25

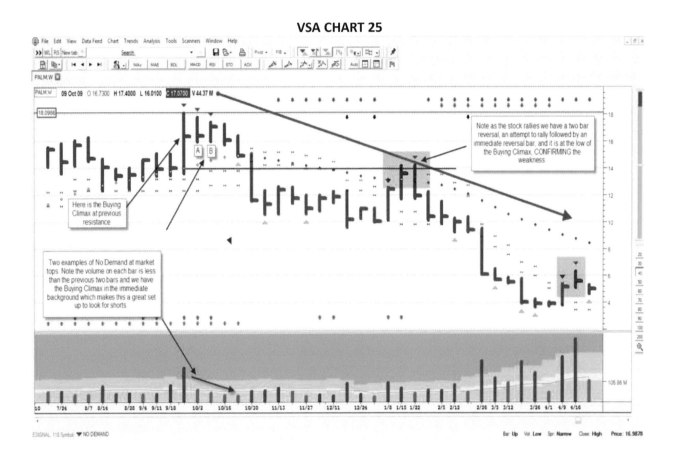

On **VSA CHART 25** we can clearly see the *No Demand* at point B (**VSA CHART 25** is the same chart as **VSA CHART 24**, just narrowed down to fewer bars).

When we see this, we should be looking for confirmation of that weakness. We can see that we have a *Two Bar Reversal* and a rejection of price at the low of the *Buying Climax*, which is marked by the first red shaded area where a red *Sign of Weakness* has appeared. At point A we have an *Up-thrust* immediately before the *No Demand,* which is very bad for higher prices.

No Demand in a Down-trend, Very Bearish!

When we see *No Demand* in a down-trend, especially after we have observed some sort of climactic action such as a *Buying Climax* or *End of a Rising Market,* then these are going to be some of the best trade set-ups to the short side.

When you see a *No Demand* bar in a down-trend do not immediately short at market, but place a sell stop a tick or two below the bottom of the *No Demand* bar. By doing this, you will avoid getting caught by Up-thrusts which will often follow a *No Demand* bar. Most traders who lose money in the markets chase the price, which means they are buying on up bars and selling on down bars, but professionals like the Smart Money do not operate like that.

High Volume means the Smart Money are very active and low Volume means the Smart Money are inactive. In a down-trend, if the Smart Money professionals become inactive as the price rises, then they are sending a signal in the charts that lower prices are coming.   That is what we call *No Demand* when we are using the Volume Spread Analysis methodology.

VSA CHART 26

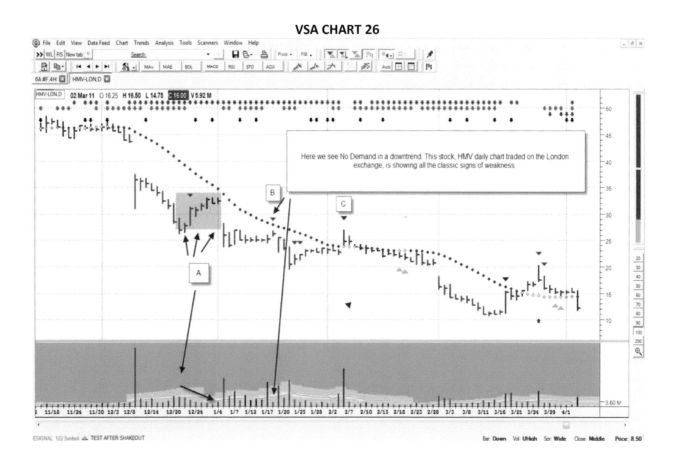

On **VSA CHART 26**, we observe the stock HMV traded on the LSE attempting to rally at point A, but just look at the Volume. There is *No Demand* where the red indicator is shown at point A, but the stock goes up for a few more days after the indicator appears and on each up bar the Volume is lighter and lighter.

Had you placed a sell order at point A, where the *No Demand* indicator has been painted in by TradeGuider and you entered your order as a sell order below the bottom of the bar as the stock gapped down six bars after the *No Demand* bar had appeared, you would have been in the trade to the short side.

We have many of our customers who trade options that are using these set-ups, as well. In this instance, a put option taken where a VSA *Sign of Weakness* appears in this strong down-trend is going to put you in the money as the stock declines in price.

I highly recommend using a stop loss order. If you had entered a short trade at point A, the stop loss would be at the high of the previous point of supply, which is the top of the price bar where you see the ultra high Volume coming in to the left of point A.

We have a secondary *No Demand* bar at point B- this is what I call a high quality *No Demand* bar. This is an up bar with a Spread that is very narrow and the Volume is clearly less than the previous two bars. The next bar has closed lower with the trend obviously moving down and this *No Demand* bar at point B re-approaching the area at point A where we saw our first *No Demand* bar. Also, we had up bars on very, very light Volume, which tells us the Smart Money was not interested in higher prices at this level previously. This up bar price action on low Volume now is confirmed by *No Demand* at point B.

At point C, we have what I call a high quality *Up-thrust* because it is in a down-trend and into the area of *No Demand* at point B. The Volume is ultra high with the bar closing near its low and the next bar closes level, confirming the selling taking place in the *Up-thrust* bar.

The Smart Money is now actively selling at this level (hence the high Volume on the *Up-thrust)* because they know this stock is weak. This is why they withdrew their interest to buy at points A and B respectively.

If you see *No Demand* before a massive *Up-thrust,* you can also place an order below the *Up-thrust*. You have confirmation of the weakness. **Always remember to look for confirmation**.

The Two Bar Reversal and Top Reversal

A *Two Bar Reversal* or *Top Reversal* is seen on the action of two bars. Sometimes we see *Top Reversals* actually causing a change in trend after a strong up-trend. A *Two Bar Reversal* that is observed at prior resistance areas is also a *Sign of Weakness,* and again, will often change any up-trend.

A *Two Bar Reversal* or *Top Reversal* is made out of an up bar (price bar closes higher than the previous bar) followed by a down bar on a wide Spread closing at, or near the low of the bar. If the Volume on the first up bar is ultra high, that means this is a very weak bar. Give more weight if the Volume is ultra high.

As we have seen, the markets work on the principle of Supply and Demand and if there is too much supply present, especially at areas of prior resistance to higher prices, then the shorting opportunities will become apparent.

The Two Bar Reversal Currency Futures 6B contract, US Dollar/UK Pound. Notice the market falls on a wide spread bar and closes near the low and takes out the closing price on the previous 20 bars. This is a two bar reversal at prior resistance.

The example shown in **VSA CHART 27** shows a *Two Bar Reversal* at previous resistance. In this example, the ultra high Volume is on the down bar is considered a very weak bar. The ultra high Volume down bar produces a red *Sign of Weakness* in the TradeGuider software program. Note that when a *Two Bar Reversal* is formed, it doesn't matter whether the ultra high Volume is on the first bar or the second bar because we can see that Smart Money players are active. When we see the close of the second bar happen below the low of the first bar, we have to conclude that there are more sellers contained in these two bars and that the ultra high Volume is showing that supply being present.

If strength appears on ultra high Volume down bars, how does the TradeGuider software correctly identify this as *Two Bar Reversal* and a *Sign of Weakness*, resulting in a significant fall in price?
Well, that is the genius of Tom Williams' invention. As I mentioned, not every ultra high Volume down bar is a sign of strength, but Tom has programmed in rules that filter the indicators based on parameters which include at what part of the trend the indicator should appear.

In this instance, this ultra high Volume bar has appeared after an up-trend and at resistance. The wide Spread down bar has wiped out the prior closing price support of the previous 20 bars.

If this ultra high Volume down bar had appeared after a down-trend in prices, especially at previous support, then this would have very likely produced a *Sign of Strength*. But in this instance, it is shown as a weak bar because of its proximity to the trend and because the indicator has seen the action of two bars. The second bar collapsing to close near the lows shows a very negative reaction to the *Effort to Rise* on the first bar. That is not something you see in a strong market.

After I see a *Two Bar Reversal*, I like to wait for confirmation as the market once again approaches the low of the second reversal bar. As you can see in the example in **VSA CHART 27**, a red indicator appears fourteen bars after point A. Can you guess what that is?

No Demand after a *Two Bar Reversal* this is a great place to take a short in harmony with the trend and approaching the low of the second reversal bar, which will now act as resistance in the future. A *Top Reversal* is seen quite rarely, but it is a very serious *Sign of Weakness* when it appears.

A *Top Reversal* happens after a long period of rising prices in a bull market. The Volume on the first bar should be ultra high, which adds to the weakness. The second bar will close lower than the bottom of the first bar. The markets work on universal laws and a *Top Reversal* shows that outcome when the effort to rally fails miserably, as observed on the close of the second bar of the reversal. This demonstrates the Effort vs. Result price dynamic.

The *Top Reversal* shows heavy supply on the first bar. When we observe the second bar closing on, or near its low, the result was a collapse in price on the second bar. The Smart Money had to be selling heavily in the high Volume up bar to the collapse and lower close of the second bar.

The market will often fall quite rapidly after this principle is seen, so it is very important that you recognize this when it appears. The news will probably be good when this appears on your chart and you will probably feel bullish, but beware, your instincts about what you are hearing in the news and in the media will mislead you. Let the chart be your guide and always remember that markets just do not like ultra high Volume coming in on up bars. Go and check your charts for yourself and you will see this is true in the majority of cases.

After you have seen a *Top Reversal,* you can go short on any ultra high Volume up bar that appears or any very low Volume up bar that appears as the down-trend begins.

Tom and I always laugh when we point this out because it sounds as though we are contradicting ourselves, specifically when we shorting on high Volume up bars and also low Volume up bars, but in fact, it is very logical. If the Smart Money is actively selling, then the Volume will be ultra high because Volume represents the activity. A few bars later, if the market attempts to go up and the Volume is now low, this tells us that there is now low activity. That is because the Smart Money would have sold on the ultra high Volume bar and are now withdrawing their interest as the price tries to rally.

Supply Coming In and Supply Overcoming Demand

In the TradeGuider software program, *Supply Coming In* is one of the most common indicators that appear which detects high and ultra high Volume on up bars (again, an up bar is one that closes higher than the preceding bar). If the Spread is wide and the very next bar closes lower, then it confirms that selling has taken place on the previous high or ultra high Volume bar, as seen on **VSA CHART 28**.

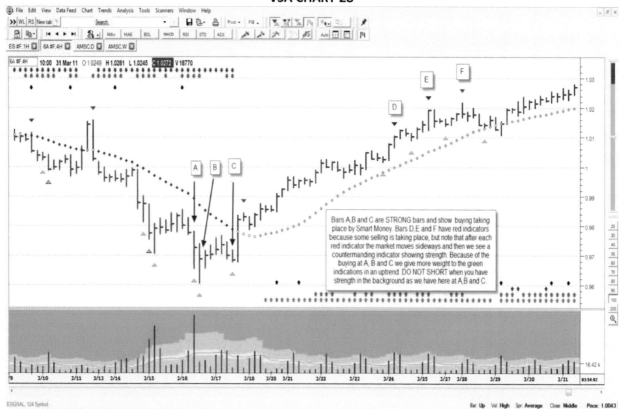

You'll see this indicator appear in up-trends, down-trends, and in sideways moving markets, but it is only a trade to the short side in a down-trend. Do not short this indicator if you see strength in the background at least 50 bars back with the market trending up. In **VSA CHART 28** we see *Supply Coming In* in an up-trend with strength in the background at points A, B, and C.

When we see strength in the background and an up-trend is clearly in place, it is inadvisable to place short trades. We see at points D and E, *Supply Coming In*. The market, which in this case is the currency futures contract 6A (the cross currency pair of the United States dollar and the Australian dollar) responds by moving sideways for a few bars, but never penetrates the low of bars D and E. We then see a countermanding indicator appear at the place where we have seen a *Sign of Weakness*, which is then almost immediately followed by a *Sign of Strength*.

The TradeGuider software is programmed to detect imbalances of supply and demand. That is why you will often see red indicators in an up-trend and green indicators in a down-trend. Since human beings are very visual we tend to see red as stop, or in the case of charts - sell, and green as go, or in the case of charts - buy. If using the TradeGuider software or our add-in studies, please remember that your best trades should be in harmony with the trend.

If you observe *Supply Coming In,* the market is in an up-trend and has signs of strong buying in the background. You will then want to watch to see if the market will subsequently *Test*. If successful, a *Test* is a *Sign of Strength*. In **VSA CHART 28**, we see *Supply Coming In* at points D and E with an *Up-thrust* at point F.

However, these are all polar bears in Hawaii! If these *Signs of Weakness* appeared in a down-trend after some climactic action showing the Smart Money selling, then these would be great short trades, but here, we have climactic buying by the Smart Money within 50 bars of the appearance of these *Signs of Weakness* with a clear up-trend in place. Also, note the low Volume down bars where the four green indicators are shown. This tells us that as the price falls, the Volume is low showing no selling pressure from the Smart Money. They are not active as the price falls because they are bullish, having bought at points A and B with having seen a very successful *Test* at point C. There has been some selling at points D, E, and F (the TradeGuider software has correctly detected that), but since there is strength in the background with a clear up-trend, these *Signs of Weakness* should not be a place to short.

VSA CHART 29

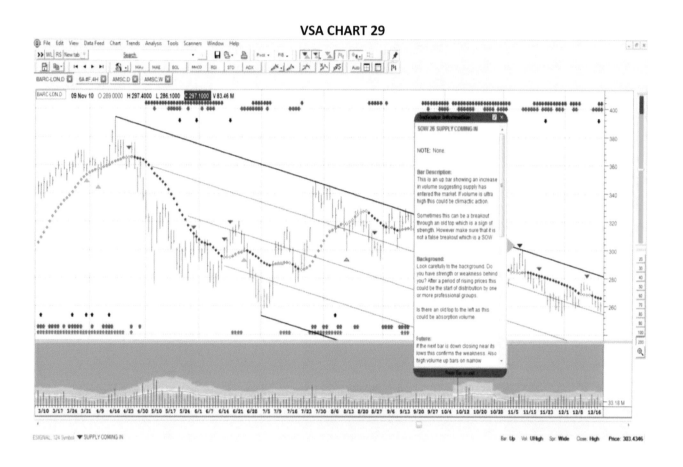

VSA CHART 29 (the daily chart of the UK FTSE 100 stock, Barclays) shows the best place to short when *Supply Coming In* appears. Note that if you are using the TradeGuider software or add-in studies, by left-clicking on the indicator, a dialogue box will pop up giving detailed information about the indicator. The indicators were written by Tom Williams with the assistance of UK professional trader and fund manager, Philip Friston, who has been successfully investing using VSA for over 20 years.

By reading these boxes, you will greatly decrease the learning time when you begin mastering the art of chart reading using VSA. Note that the indicator for *Supply Coming In* is at the top of the down-trend channel of the chart. This indicator is confirmed because the very next bar closes lower than the indicator bar. It is a polar bear in the Arctic - it is in the right place! High or ultra high Volume bars in a down-trend should get your attention, especially if they are at the top of a down-trend channel.

If you remember that the Smart Money sell into up bars, it'll serve you well whatever you trade.

When I see *Supply Coming In,* as with many of the VSA *Signs of Weakness*, I want to see the market move below the low of the bar on which the weakness has appeared. If I see a sign of weakness and the market moves sideways plus we subsequently see *No Supply* or *Tests*, then this is a sign that the market is not ready for a decline and may indeed have another leg up.

Tom taught me that a trend in price often goes on a lot longer than you may think, that is why trading in harmony with the overall trend on at least three time frames will often keep you out of poor trades.

The End of a Rising Market

This is my favorite indicator. Although quite rare, when you see it, you know the bull move that will accompany this indicator is coming to an end and the selling by the Smart Money is taking place aggressively. When this indicator appears on a weekly chart of a stock or commodity, the news that will accompany this indicator will be very good. Everyone will be bullish and looking to get into the market, when in fact, they should be looking to go short.

You will see this indicator on smaller time frames, even a 1 minute chart. If you see *No Demand* after you have seen the *End of a Rising Market,* this will confirm the weakness. Please see **VSA CHART 3** (JP Morgan) for a good example.

The Volume accompanying this set-up will be ultra high and most importantly, the Spread of the price bar will be narrow. The price should close in the middle of the bar- it will be an up bar, which will close higher than the preceding bar.

This bar should be into *Fresh New Ground*. **What we mean by *Fresh New Ground* is that there should be no price action within a minimum of 500 bars.** Also, there shouldn't be any old resistance levels because the chart has made new highs. I have seen the *End of a Rising Market* indicator appear at old resistance levels that worked extremely well to the short side.

The narrow range of the bar is caused by the mass of sell orders from the Smart Money satisfying the rush of buy orders from the unsuspecting Herd. As prices go up day by day or minute by minute (depending on your chart and time frame), the Herd fear missing out on this never ending bull move. They think this bull move is really occurring, so they buy at these market tops. This indicator often causes the market to move sideways for several bars, but then suddenly you will get what I call the *Gotcha bar*. This is a high Volume bar with a wide Spread that closes on the low near the bottom of the bar and takes out many of the previous support levels that were observed in the bullish move.

Since this set-up appears when everyone is bullish, it catches many, many traders and investors and costs them a lot of money. Remember, the chart never lies, so do not trust your gut instinct, do not trust what you hear or read in the media, ignore the rumors and supposedly 'hot tips' that will be coming at you from various quarters. To put it simply, just trust your chart.

If we could chart the housing market in the United States in late 2009, we would have seen two very clear VSA principles, the *End of a Rising Market* followed by lots of *No Demand*, and then it would collapse in prices.

That is exactly how this works in the stock market, futures market, commodities market and even the Forex market. An ultra high Volume up bar on a narrow Spread into *Fresh New Ground* accompanied by very good news about the instrument being traded is a signal from the Smart Money. It is an alert that they are selling what they bought previously at much lower prices. Ignore this signal at your peril!

To short this, wait for the market to turn and look for the *Gotcha bar* that confirms the weakness, and then you can short on any *No Demand* bars or *Up-thrust* that you identify. The TradeGuider software has a scanner that scans for VSA indicators of strength and weakness, so if you see a cluster of indicators at the right edge of the chart and *End of a Rising Market* is one of them, you have a very profitable short opportunity awaiting you. While everyone around you is buying, you will be sitting back, smiling quietly, just waiting for that *Gotcha bar* to trigger the short trade set-up.

CHAPTER 7
Key Principles of the VSA Methodology
Part 2: Strength

The Shakeout

A *Shakeout* does exactly what the indicator name describes. It shakes out as many traders/investors as possible before a bull move takes place. It is a powerful *Sign of Strength*. *Shakeout*s are used as an opportunity by the Smart Money to dislodge traders who are in a long position and trigger as many stops as possible.

The *Shakeout* will often mislead many traders who see the widespread down bar. It is often viewed as a *Sign of Weakness* and will most likely be accompanied by bad news, but in fact, it is a *Sign of Strength*.

The biggest *Shakeout* we observed during 2010 was the May 6th Flash Crash, but what was interesting about this *Shakeout* is that it was not accompanied by any bad news on that day. In fact, we saw that even the mainstream media had great difficulty trying to make sense of what happened, as evidenced by the comments of Maria Bartiromo on CNBC that day. However, what we indeed witnessed on the 6th of May was a perfect example of a *Shakeout* accompanied by ultra high Volume. In actuality, the highest Volume seen during 2010 was seen on 6th May Flash Crash day.

So how do we trade a *Shakeout?*

A *Shakeout* will often occur after an accumulation phase has begun. Accumulation is simply the Smart Money buying the underlying instrument at lower prices because they have seen an opportunity. Accumulation in any market will take time.

An opportunity arises where the market can be marked down for buying. The Smart Money will absorb any traders that are being shaken out and are selling. They will buy into the panic selling. The ultra high Volume that accompanies a *Shakeout* is showing us that both the Smart Money and the Herd are active. This is creating the ultra high Volume.

Remember that whenever we see ultra high Volume, whether it is on an up bar or a down bar, supply will still be present. This supply will need to be tested in the future before the market begins the bull move. Often after an initial *Shakeout,* the market actually falls further and we start to see *Stopping Volume* and then *No Supply*. If we look at the *Shakeout* in the Dow on May 6th we can observe these principles in action. See **VSA CHART 30**.

VSA CHART 30

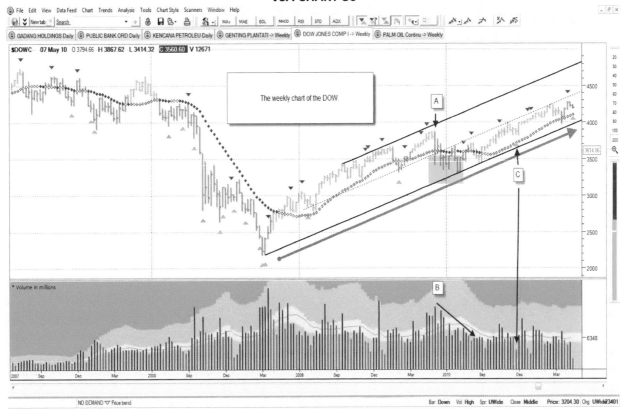

In the weekly **VSA CHART 30,** we can clearly see that the Dow is in a strong weekly up-trend prior to the *Shakeout* at point A, which is the week of the Flash Crash. The area highlighted in green is very important because we see that after the *Shakeout* week, the market indeed falls, but as it falls over the next six weeks (note the Volume) it is getting lighter and lighter as the Smart Money withdraw their interest in lower prices. That is because they have shaken out the market and they fully expect higher prices.

In fact, the Dow rallied nearly a thousand points within a year despite all the bad news about the economy and world troubles. In many of my past webinars and live seminars, I polled the audience and nearly all were bearish during this time. The Smart Money players were bullish and they were buying at lower prices. **Remember, the Smart Money buy on down bars!**

When you see a *Shakeout*, it is your early warning that the Smart Money is active. *Shakeout*s work best if you are already in an up-trend since all the buying or accumulation has already taken place. I like to look at the trend on the larger time frame that I am trading, and in stocks or indices I start with the weekly trend and put a trend channel in place. On **VSA CHART 30** we see at point C a perfect entry to go long. It is a down bar on this weekly chart, but this bar is very important because it meets the following criteria to buy:

- Price action is now above the high of the *Shakeout* at bar A. This is important because as price action penetrates the top of the *Shakeout* bar, we can conclude that the Smart Money is now in control and are ready for higher prices.

- The overall trend is up.

- Bar C is a down bar.

- Bar C has a narrow spread.

- The Volume is the lowest seen for several months. In fact, it is ultra low. Due to the *Shakeout* in the background this now becomes very bullish. Volume is activity. This low activity is a tell-tale sign that the Smart Money are not interested in lower prices.

- The very next bar closes up, which is also important because it is confirming the strength. The next bar is up on what I call healthy Volume. It is high, but not ultra high, and seen after bar C.

You will note that the VSA principle, which is *No Supply,* appears on the weekly chart in late November. Is there an entry on the daily chart that can give us a buy set-up a little earlier to increase our profit potential?

In **VSA CHART 31**, we get a clear set of principles that give a great entry to go long at point F.

VSA CHART 31

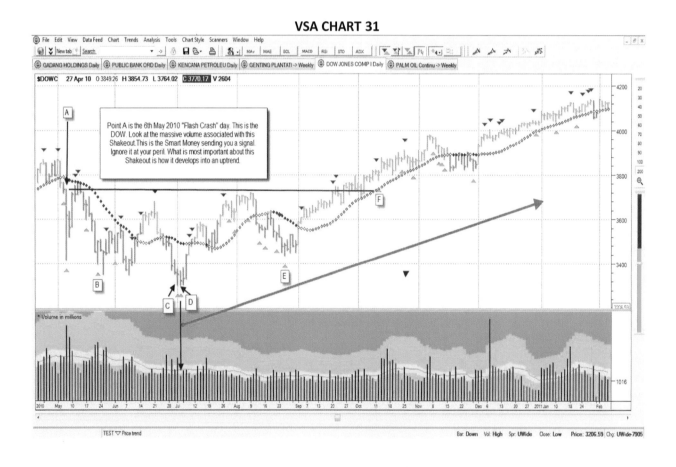

Let's go through each bar from point A, which is the May 6th Flash Crash. We note that after the *Shakeout,* the market continues to fall on both the daily and weekly chart. This is very common as sellers continue to sell or leave the market. They have been totally confused by their losses and sell what they have left. You can see the Smart Money continue to absorb this selling and then at point B, we have a *Test* after a *Shakeout*. The *Test,* in this case, is on high Volume and because the Volume is high, the market will fall into another leg to point C. Again, the Volume is fairly high on this day, but at point D we get a clear low Volume *Test* of a *Shakeout*. That is what you want to look for- a low Volume *Test*. It is confirmed because the next bar has closed as an up bar, a price bar that has closed higher than the low Volume *Test*.

At this point, would this be the place to buy?

No. This is because we can see that the market is still trending down towards the bottom of the trend channel and we want to buy in an up-trend, not when the trend is down.

Do we have customers who take risk at these areas?

Yes, we do and as you get more experienced with Volume Spread Analysis, you may well want to take aggressive trades, but first, I want to teach you high probability/low risk entries, which means you will have to be patient and wait for the principle to set-up.

At point E, we make a higher low and start to attempt to trend up, but we have not yet exceeded the high of the *Shakeout* at bar A. Can you mark the Closing Price of the *Shakeout* bar and wait for that to be tested in order to go long from there?

Yes, the difference is that it is just more aggressive. I like to wait for the market to move above the top of the *Shakeout* bar and then either look for a *Test* that is successful with the next bar closing up, a *No Supply* bar, or a *Test in a Rising Market.*

At bar F, we have everything that meets my criteria for a long trade. We have a test that is successful and above the high of the *Shakeout* bar.

Note that I also have at least 5 green diamonds and 5 green bars that show me the TradeGuider software indicating that an up-trend is forming. The *Shakeout* in the background makes it a very good entry to buy or go long. As you will see in **VSA CHART 33**, the same principle that I have shown in the futures market (JPY/USD) contract appear in the 4 hour time frame of the spot forex chart. We see *Shakeouts* followed by *No Supply* very often in the major currency pairings. Since, these contracts are so liquid, the resulting moves can be very profitable.

At The Best of Wyckoff seminar that we held in Florida in June of 2010, I had already voiced that I was bullish about the market because of the *Shakeout.* I fully expected higher prices. If you visit www.thebestofwyckoff.com, you can view the videos including my presentation where I talk about the *Shakeout* before it even happened. I realize that many traders and investors often think it is easy to read charts in hindsight, but if the VSA principle is there in hindsight, it must have been there at the right edge of the chart. Unless you know what to look out for, you may be a little contrarian and therefore miss the opportunity.

Fortunately, we do live trading sessions and record all our presentations about the current market conditions in our VSA Club. Tom Williams and Fund Manager, Philip Friston run the VSA Club. We have regular guest speakers, including world-renowned Wyckoff experts, David Weis and Dr. Gary Dayton. In the VSA Club, real trading accounts are used during our demonstrations and we call the markets out live, usually in foresight.

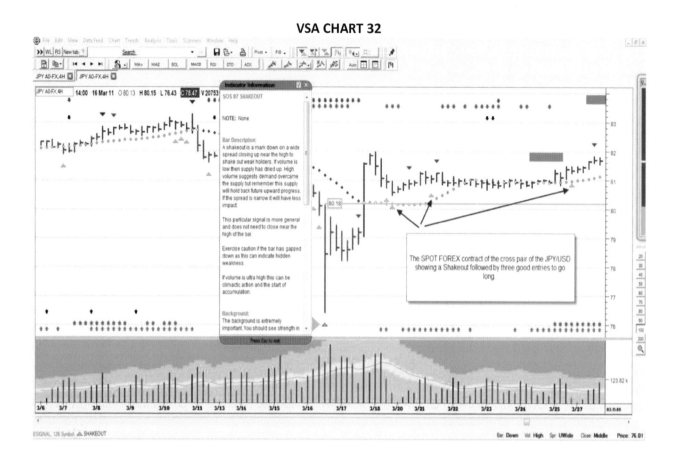

Remember, a *Shakeout* can occur in any market and in any time frame, including the forex market where they are very common. Then, after you see that *Shakeout,* do not forget to wait and see how the market responds. If the market moves sideways and moves above the top of the *Shakeout* bar, higher prices can be expected. A *Shakeout* on a long time frame, such as a weekly chart, will have a dramatic effect on price, like what we observed after the May 6th giant *Shakeout.*

No Supply and Test in a Rising Market

No Supply and a *Test in a Rising Market* are my favorite indicators to go long, but there are important rules I apply to my strategy before entering a trade:

- There must be a clear up-trend in place in at least three time frames if trading intraday and at least two time frames if trading end of day. As a guide, I use the daily and weekly for stocks and commodities end of day. If trading forex intraday I use the 4 hour, the 1 hour, and 15 minute charts. For trading futures such as the E-mini's, I use a 30 minute, 15 minute, and 5 minute chart for the E-mini Dow and S&P. The exception is when trading the NASDAQ I use the 15 minute, 9 minute, and 3 minute charts because the NQ often leads the market and moves quicker.

- There must be a clear sign of strength showing the Smart Money buying in the background. For the background, I usually go back at least 50 price bars in my time frames, paying most attention to the largest time frame first and looking for my entry on the smallest time frame. If I see a *Selling Climax*, *Bag Holding*, or a violent *Shakeout* on ultra high Volume, then this confirms strength in the background and will add to the overall strength in the market.

- If using the TradeGuider software or add-in studies, I want to see at least 5 green short term trending diamonds and 5 medium term up-trend bars in at least two time frames. Again, note that you can change the color of the bars. I use blue bars in my TradeGuider RT program and green bars in my TradeGuider EOD program.

- The market must have moved above the top of the *Climactic Bar,* regardless of whether it is a *Shakeout,* a *Selling Climax,* or *Bag Holding.*

- The *No Supply* bar will be a down bar. The Volume will be low, or even better, ultra low.

- The next bar will be an up bar on an increase in Volume. The Volume will be average or high, but not ultra high. If the Volume is ultra high, expect to see further testing before the market moves up.

I do not place a market order when I see a *No Supply* bar. I place a buy order a few ticks above the *No Supply* bar and I let the market come to me. It is actually the very opposite of shorting on *No Demand.* In fact you will observe that all the *Signs of Strength* are the inverse of the *Signs of Weakness.* If you observed a chart that was full of weak bars and turned it upside down, the weak bars would now look like strong bars when using VSA principles. **VSA CHART 33** shows a clear *No Supply* bar that is in the right place.

VSA CHART 33

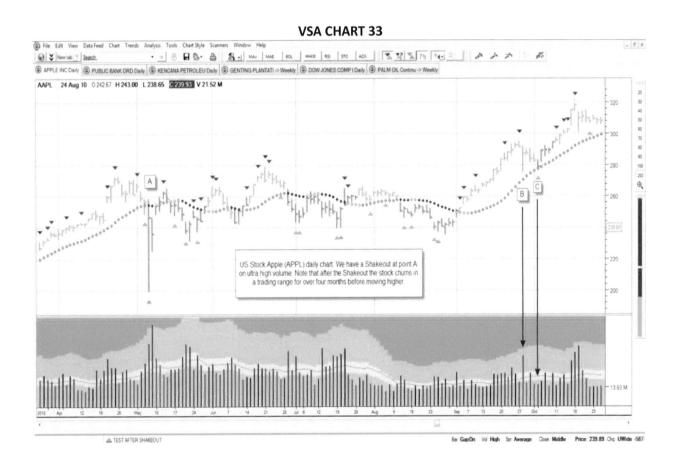

US Stock Apple (APPL) daily chart. We have a Shakeout at point A on ultra high volume. Note that after the Shakeout the stock churns in a trading range for over four months before moving higher

At point A, we have an ultra high Volume *Shakeout.* The Spread of the *Shakeout* is massive and the Closing Price is on the high. There is strength on this bar that will need to be tested and you will see that as a result, the stock churned for four months. Churning is very common after an ultra high Volume bar appears.

The Smart Money players bring the price back down into the range of the *Shakeout* bar for more buying to test the supply, seen at point A, and also on the bar immediately after point A. This is why we see some ultra high Volume down bars and low Volume down bars.

At point B, we have an ultra high Volume down bar. The very next bar closes as an up bar, showing us there is more buying going on at bar B. At bar C, we see a classic example of a *No Supply* bar. It is a down bar (a price bar that has closed lower than the bar behind it) and the Spread of the bar is narrow. The Closing Price is on the low of the bar near the bottom. The Volume is ultra low and most importantly, the Volume is less than the previous two bars. The next bar closes higher on a healthy increase in Volume, but not ultra high Volume.

I have the TradeGuider diamond trending system and bar color trending system both green and meeting my criteria. This is a great trade set-up to buy the market and go long, but remember, when we see a *No Supply* bar, place the order a few ticks above the bar and let the market come to you.

This is now a polar bear in the Arctic because you have strength on the *Shakeout* bar. The *No Supply* bar is in the right place. As you can see, the Apple stock rallied from this bar to a new high of $364.90 from the indicator bar, which closed at $278.64. Remember that this principle is a high probability long trade when you have a serious *Sign of Strength* in the background.

Bag Holding

If you ever see the *Bag Holding* indicator appear, it is a very powerful *Sign of Strength*, but note it is fairly rare. This is the exact opposite of the *End of a Rising Market*, which of course, is a *Sign of Weakness*. This indicator will appear after you have observed a bear market or have seen a dramatic fall in price on the instrument you are trading. There should be a very clear down-trend in place. If the market is gapped down when this indicator appears, then this just adds to the strength. The Spread of the bar will be narrow and the price will close in the middle or high of the bar with the Volume being ultra high. Some bad news will accompany this indicator if trading stocks or commodities.

What is happening is that the Smart Money has seen a great opportunity, which is often news driven, to buy an instrument at prices that are now extremely attractive. The Herd will be panic selling due to the news and the Smart Money will be buying into all the selling, which caps the bottom of the market. This causes the narrow Spread (range) on the bar and the close will be in the middle or towards the high.

For every sell order coming into the exchange, a buy order from the Smart Money is satisfying that order. This is very bullish. This will often result in an immediate change in trend. As a word of caution, on the majority of occasions, *No Supply* or *Testing* may very well follow subsequently.

If Tom Williams sees *Bag Holding,* he would immediately go long. As for me, I wait for a definite change in trend followed by a *No Supply* bar or a *Test in a Rising Market.*

Selling Climax

A *Selling Climax* is a very powerful *Sign of Strength*. After a period of falling prices in a bear market, a point will be reached where the Herd can no longer stand being locked in as the price continues to fall. They will want to get out with minimum loss. The news will be negative, usually very bad, and the market will plummet down quickly. At this point, prices are now attractive to the Smart Money and they will begin to buy, or accumulate, at these low levels.

This is called a *Selling Climax* because in order to initiate this, you have to have a mass of selling from traders or investors who are locked in high price levels where they bought the market and are now showing a loss. We call these losing traders or investors, *weak holders*.

It is interesting how we can observe crowd behavior by simply looking at a chart. It is uncanny how at certain price levels, we see a clear exchange from weak holders to the Smart Money, who at this point will be the *strong* holders. As mentioned in the previous example of the British Petroleum (BP) chart, the low that was observed in 2003 was seen again during the BP Gulf of Mexico oil spill disaster.

The Smart Money rushed in and bought at the 2003 accumulation level. This happened during the week the mainstream media told us that BP had failed to cap the well. This very unfortunate news was based on the rumor that BP may go out of business or be taken over by the Libyans, which was enough to convince any trader or investor holding BP to dump the stock, even if it meant taking a loss. This is exactly what the Smart Money relies on.

Please refer back to the BP chart in the Chapter 4. This is a classic example of a *Selling Climax.* The news that surrounded the event is very well documented as is the result on the BP stock price after the *Selling Climax* was observed. The stock price rallied from its low of $26.83 to a high of $49.50 in just over six months. This proves that the Smart Money, indeed, buys on bad news. Thusly, when the chart gives you one of these set-ups, you will need to ignore what you see and hear. Trust your chart. Your chart will not let you down if you learn to read it correctly.

Stopping Volume

Stopping Volume will appear very frequently, especially on your intraday charts. It does exactly what it says- it stops the market at the point you see it. There are three different types of *Stopping Volume*:

- In an *up-trend* where buying has been observed in the background: this is **bullish.**

- In a *down-trend* where selling or weakness is in the background: this is **bearish.**

- In a *ranging market* with subsequent price action that stops the market from falling to a certain support level, can be considered bullish, but it is more difficult to trade. I would consider this **neutral.**

Let's first look at *Stopping Volume* in a strong up-trend with strength in the background on **CHART VSA 34**.

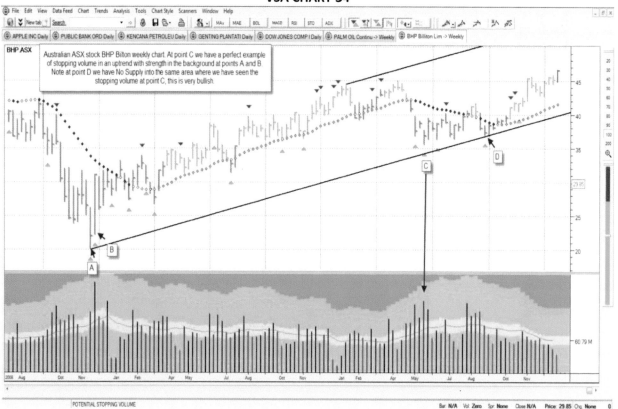

Stopping Volume in an Up-trend

As we can see on **VSA CHART 34**, we have two serious *Signs of Strength* at points A and B, which change the trend into an up-trend. At point C, we see an ultra high Volume down bar with a narrow Spread along with the close in the middle. This is *Stopping Volume* in an up-trend where buying has been observed in the background. This is bullish. The next bar closes higher and the Volume is ultra high, which is why the stock falls back down into this area at point D, where we now have *No Supply*.

If you had bought at point C and placed a buy order a few ticks above bar C, your trade would have been triggered and you would not have been stopped out. This is because the strength at points A and B shows the strong up-trend in place and the *Stopping Volume* was confirmed when the next bar closed higher.

You have put the odds in your favor of a successful long trade by observing what the chart is telling you. Often, this will happen on some sort of negative news about the stock in order to fool you into thinking it is going to fall, but if all the Volume had been selling Volume on bar C, how could the next bar close higher?

If we look at the news on May 21st, 2010, which is the day this indicator appeared, it was not good news. The Australian Government was proposing a super tax on the Australian resources sector and the press release even states, "This could put prosperity and employment prospects of all Australians at risk."

That is not good news at all and the stock gaps down on that day. However, when you can read the chart, you can clearly see the buying that happened at points A and B. Remember, beware of the news and be contrarian. I can assure you, it will make you money.

Stopping Volume in a Down-trend

We will now look at *Stopping Volume* in a down-trend on **VSA CHART 35**, where we will see selling, or weakness, in the background. In any market where you observe a strong down-trend in place, do not attempt to go long or buy the market. Just because a green indicator appears in the TradeGuider software or add-in study does not mean buy, **unless it is in the right place**.

VSA CHART 35

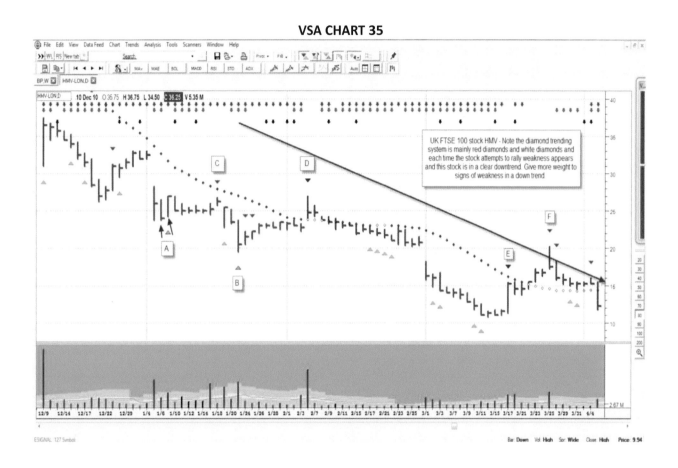

At point A, we see a green indicator that appears on an up bar, which is unusual. That is because this indicator is actually looking at the bar prior to bar A and bar A, itself. This is *Stopping Volume,* but it is also a polar bear in Hawaii- it is in the wrong place. There is a *Climactic Action* bar at the very left of the chart that had *Tests* that followed it failing miserably, which of itself, is a serious *Sign of Weakness*.

The indicator at bar A results in the stock moving sideways for a few days. At bar C, we have a *No Demand* bar that is in the right place because we have serious weakness in the background. Here, we are in a strong down-trend on the weekly and daily charts. Each time the stock attempts to rally, we see *No Demand* bars, *Up-thrusts*, and *Supply Coming In*, which is not good for higher prices.

At point B, further *Stopping Volume* appears and actually causes the stock to rally temporarily, but this is countermanded by more weakness on bar D. This clearly shows that supply is coming in. In fact, that is a great set-up to short, as we have previously seen in the *Signs of Weakness*. *Stopping Volume* in a down-trend will often cause the market to go sideways for a few bars, or even go up for a few bars. Also note that if you take a long position, you are swimming against the tide and I strongly advise against it. To make money in the markets, you must look for higher probability, lower risk entries, and if you are patient, they will arrive most definitely.

Finally, in this section on *Stopping Volume,* we will look at *Stopping Volume* in a ranging market, stopping the market falling at a certain support level.

VSA CHART 36

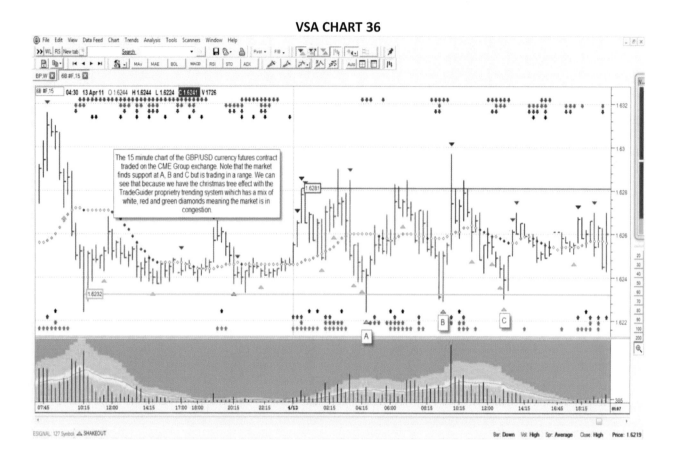

In **VSA CHART 36**, we can clearly see the market is bouncing off support marked at A, B, and C, or the green support line, and being sold again at the red resistance line. At point A, we have a high Volume bar that closes on the highs, but is still considered a down bar because it is a price bar that closes lower than the preceding bar. The next bar closes up showing the buying at bar A, which the TradeGuider software reads as a *Shakeout.* At bar B, we observe over two bars, *Stopping Volume*, which is a two bar indicator, and again, the market moves higher back up to resistance.

These two bars look very similar to a *Bottom Reversal,* but they are not at the bottom of a down-trend. They are correctly shown as *Stopping Volume* bars by the TradeGuider software program as seen in **VSA CHART 37**. At Bar C, we again find support and *Strength Coming In*, which is a very similar indicator to *Stopping Volume*. The bar at C closes in the middle and the Volume is now average. The next bar closes higher again, on average Volume, and the market responds by going back up towards the resistance. It does not get there because of the ultra high Volume, wide Spread up bar that closes in the middle between bars B and C. This is a serious *Sign of Weakness*.

Is going long at these support levels a high probability, low risk trade?

In my opinion, it is not, but we have a number of customers who trade these set-ups using tight stops just below the support line.

Tests

The following excerpt is taken from the weekly newsletter produced by Tom Williams in the VSA Club. It is an excellent introduction to *Testing,* a principle of the VSA methodology that can initially be confusing because *Tests* can appear in various bar formations, including down bar *Tests* and up bar *Tests:*

*We have many requests to explain **Testing**. The principle of a **Test** is very simple.*

All markets move on supply and demand. Professional money will find it difficult to mark up an instrument that they are interested in until they are sure that during their mark-up, it will not be swamped by supply (selling) coming in because it will cost them dearly. One of the best ways to check this is to mark the market down, which will normally encourage those that would want to sell, to sell.

*However, if the Volume is low, especially when the Spread is narrow and probably closing in the middle, it tells the professional operator that at that moment in time, there is no selling to worry about. You see this **Test** very frequently and it can often give you a great opportunity to go long.*

Testing will always initially happen on a down bar.

*It has to be on a down bar to tempt any trader that is going to sell, to sell. With that said, you will see many Tests on up bars. The reason is because, initially, on a smaller time frame the **Test** was, in fact, on a down bar, but as the professionals could see, there was no **Supply Coming In**, so they jumped in on the trade going for higher prices.*

*Now if you come along using a higher time frame and because of the surge of buying on the lower time frame the market has actually rallied up, which will the impression that the **Test** is on an up bar. But even on an up bar it will have the characteristic signs of a **Test**. That is what we call a **Longer Term Test of Supply**.*

*You often see support coming into a market, which may be **Stopping Volume**, or **Climactic Action**. The market rallies somewhat, then arches over, to then slowly drop back down into the area where the initial **Signs of Strength** seen as **Stopping Volume** or **Climactic Action**, were seen. Now as the market falls back down into an area in where to the left there was high Volume, the Volume is now low, which is clearly indicating that the supply has in fact been absorbed. The market is now ready for a bull move and this is seen very frequently.*

As Tom has stated above, *Tests* can occur on both down bars, as well as on up bars. I think Tom's explanation of the different time frames explains exactly why this occurs. In a *Test*, we are interested in knowing:

- Whether it is a good place to go long.

- Whether it is a time not to trade at all.

- If it fails, whether it a *Sign of Weakness*.

In order to do this, let's first look at the different types of *Tests* that are used in the VSA methodology. They can be arranged into three categories:

- **Bullish**
  -Test in a Rising Market
  -Test after a Shakeout
  -Test after Up-thrust
  -Test after Strength in an Up-trend

- **Bearish**
  -Failed Test
  -Test after Weakness in a Down-trend

- **Neutral**
  -Basic Test
  -Test of Breakout
  -Tests into Areas of High Supply
  -Tests after Weakness in an Up-trend

Now that we've grouped these *Tests*, it is very important to grasp the concept of a *Test*.

A *Test*, of course, is a trial, assessment, or examination of something. In the case of VSA it is the Smart Money testing for supply.

Remember, if there is too much supply, prices will fall. If the Smart Money is bullish, they will want to ensure that the supply has been removed or absorbed before commencing an up move.

Something you will see very often, when a market is ready for a change in trend from a down-trend to an up-trend, is an extremely ultra high Volume down bar. For example, a *Selling Climax* that causes the market to stop and then start to rally up. You will see that after a few bars, the market will retrace and price action will go into the area where we previously saw the *Climactic Action* bar. If the Volume is still fairly high on this secondary down bar, but the Volume is actually lower than the Volume on the Climactic Action bar, then this can be seen as a ***High Volume Test***.

The Characteristic 'W' Shape

The result of a *High Volume Test* is often another attempt to rally with yet another retracement back into the price action of the *Climactic Action* bar. Note that this time we are looking for much lower Volume than on the previous two retracements, which causes a characteristic 'W' shape to the bottom of the chart.

However, keep in mind that the market you are trading may retrace several times before it makes the up move as shown in **VSA CHART 38**. As long as each retracement is on low Volume, this is a good sign that higher prices are coming.

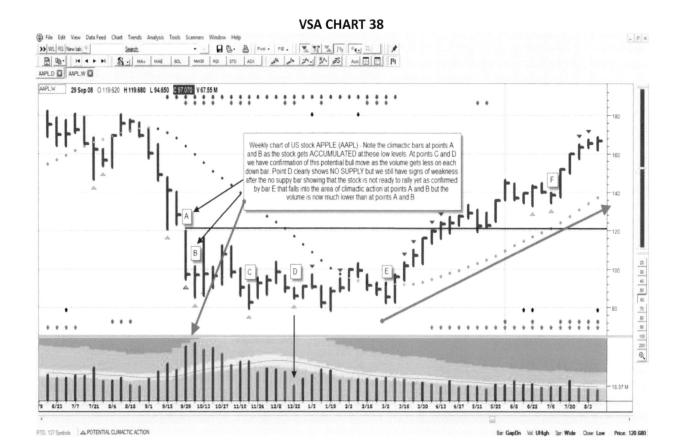

VSA CHART 38 shows *Climactic Action* at bar A and a *Selling Climax* at bar B on this weekly chart of the US stock, APPLE. Bar C falls below bar B, but the Volume is lower than at bars A and B. However, the Volume is still quite high at bar C, so the market fails to rally. We get a clear indication that a bull move is setting up, since we have a *No Supply* bar at point D. Subsequently, we see two *Signs of Weakness.*

That means that the stock is not ready to rally just yet and we must be patient. The stock falls into the same price action area as bars A, B, and C, shown at point E, but now the Volume is a lot lower than at points A, B and C. Now the rally begins and the highest probability entry to go long is at bar F, which is a *Test* in exactly the right place. Why is it in the right place? Why is it a good entry to go long?

It is because bar F meets the following criteria:

- We have serious strength in the background on bars A and B, which is confirmed at bars D and E.

- The stock breaks the high of bar A, which was the start of the *Climactic Action* and now, since the price action has moved above the top of bar A, we can infer that the buyers are now moving this stock upwards (if the stock were weak, it would hardly have the energy to move above bar A).

- We have at least 5 green diamonds and 5 blue bars showing that the stock is in an up-trend (if using the TradeGuider system).

- We see a very good example of a *Test* at bar F. It is a down bar, the Spread of the bar is narrow, and the Volume is low.

- Most importantly, the next bar after bar F closes higher on an increase in Volume, but not excessive or ultra high Volume. Due to the strength in the background and the up-trend now clearly in place, this is a high probability entry to buy this stock.

Remember this trade set-up applies to any market and any time frame, even though I am showing this on a weekly stock chart. *Tests* are a great place to go long in any market if you see strong bars in the background, as shown in **VSA CHART 38**. Always remember to place a buy order above the test bar a few ticks. Do not buy at market on a *Test* because a *Test* can sometimes fail. If you had gone long at market on the *Test*, you would now be under pressure as the market falls. Furthermore, a *Test* is deemed successful when the next bar closes higher than the *Test* bar. By placing a buy order above the *Test,* you are actually buying as the *Test* is confirming.

We will now examine a serious *Sign of Weakness* that gets tested, which actually results in a bullish move. I cover this trade in great detail on the TradeGuider YouTube channel, which was a *No Demand* of an *Up-thrust* in the daily chart of Silver (SLV) on the 9th of November, 2010. I was looking for a short trade set-up, but that set-up never came. The *Sign of Weakness* was tested and we were still in an up-trend. This is a good example of why some *Signs of Weakness* turn out non- bearish, if they are not confirmed.

As Tom stated in his book *"Master the Markets"*, trends go on a lot longer than you expect. For a short trade in this market, I would have needed to see a *Gotcha bar* followed by *No Demand* bars as the market fell through the low of bar A, as shown on **VSA CHART 39** at the red line. As the market re-approached that line on low Volume up bars, I would have seen that bar A had been confirmed as a very weak bar by the *No Demand* bars, but that never happened. In fact the market continued to move higher after we saw the initial *Test* at bar B, which was on fairly high Volume.

VSA CHART 39

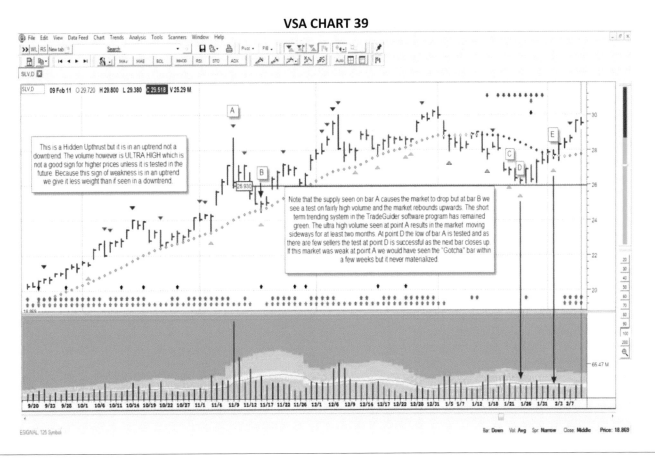

On **VSA CHART 39**, at bars C and D, I get confirmation that this market is not ready to fall. It is preparing for another phase up to encourage more buyers and bar D is testing the low of bar A to draw out any sellers. Note how low the Volume is on bar D as the market approaches the low of bar A. Remember, Volume is **activity**.

On these down days, the Volume is low because the Smart Money are not actively selling into the falling price, but instead are seeing if there are any sellers at this level. If any of the large institutions, big banks were actively selling here; we would see their footprints in the Volume. Low Volume on these down bars show lack of supply, where there was supply showing at bar A.

At bar E we have our strongest *Test* yet and a clear indication that there is *No Supply* in this market. The market rallies away from the low of bar A and the Volume we see at bar E is some of the lowest Volume on the chart. Note the very narrow Spread of the bar at point E and note that it is also a down bar. It is confirmed when the next bar closes up.

Since we did not see a complete reversal of the trend after bar A, and instead, we observed that the market appears to churn and move in a range for several weeks and then come down to *Test* several times, we can infer that this market is not ready for a sell-off. At this point, we look for long positions as the market rallies.

If you see a serious *Sign of Weakness,* you must wait for the market to confirm that the weakness you see is causing a reaction to the downside. **Do not just look at one bar in isolation, but look at the complete picture as the market unfolds.** If the market fails to change trend and constantly *Tests* as it moves sideways after a *Sign of Weakness* has appeared, that means the Smart Money has seen an opportunity for higher prices. It will be good for them to sell at these higher prices since they would have bought at much lower prices.

Test in a Rising Market

My favorite entry to go long is a *Test in a Rising Market*. It is one of the easiest to see.

I have traded in a number of traders' challenges at various traders' expos around the United States and I specifically remember the 2010 competition at the New York Traders Expo where I took a live trade using a *Test in a Rising Market* while trading the CME Group E-mini NASDAQ.

Trading solo with 100% focus in your own environment is daunting enough, but trading in front of thousands of other traders who are watching live and online, just waiting for you to make a stupid mistake or lose money is the ultimate challenge for any trader- especially since we're trading with real money! It is little wonder they call it The Traders Challenge!

Tom has always taught me to be patient. Also, when you become confident in your trade set-ups as I am, you'll know immediately when a high probability trade set-up is in front of you. At that New York Traders Expo in February, I had to wait over an hour for the set-up!

Tom compared this to waiting for the right bus to arrive before jumping on board. What he means by that is trust in your VSA analysis and principles so very obvious high probability, low risk entries will arrive. For example, if I want to ensure that I arrive at the right destination and I know I need to take bus number 53 north, then I would be stupid to jump on a number 15 south to take me in the wrong direction!

Many traders and investors do not want to wait for the right trade, so they end up jumping on the wrong bus! Then they wonder why they are consistently losing money, blowing up their accounts, and going in the wrong direction.

The principles you are learning from this book will appear in every market and in every time frame where we can get the Volume, the Spread, and the Closing Price from the data, as well as some historical data.

A *Test in a Rising Market* is a very good trade set-up to go long, but it must meet the following criteria to be a high probability trade to the long side:

- There must be a clear up-trend in place in at least 3 time frames (you'll learn more about time frames in a later chapter about developing a VSA trading plan).

- There should be a clear sign of *Climactic Buying* in the larger time frame, such as a *Shakeout, Bag Holding,* or a *Selling Climax.*

- The *Test in a Rising Market* will be on a down bar with a narrow Spread along with the Closing Price on the low of the bar.

- The open and body of the **test bar** should not penetrate the preceding bar.

- The Volume should be very low, the lower the better. High Volume *Tests* seen in rising markets often come back and get re-tested at the same level. So if you are long, you may see a small rise in price before the re-test of the *High Volume Test*. Be aware of this.

- After a *Test in a Rising Market,* the next bar should close higher than the *Test* bar.

- If using the TradeGuider software, you should have at least 5 medium term up-trend bars in at least two time frames and 5 short-term diamond trending system diamonds in at least two time frames.

VSA CHART 40 shows a daily chart of US stock, Amazon. Although I am showing this set-up on a daily stock chart, it works extremely well in small time frames, as do all the trade set-ups that are identified by VSA. Many traders and investors I meet have trouble with this concept.

They say to me, "Gavin, how can a set-up that is showing up on a weekly chart be at all relevant for me to use when scalping the E-mini S&P futures contract using a 3 minute time frame?"

At first, I had trouble with this concept myself, until I started trading the futures markets intraday. Now I can say I traded live at the New York Traders Expo using these same set-ups! I used my favorite set-up to go long using the 3 minute, 5 minute and 15 minute time frames to determine my optimal entry and exit, trading the E-mini NASDAQ.

Tom had developed these trade set-ups that he used as a stock trader, years before computers were invented and that is the reason that VSA is so robust and will work in any time frame. This is because the analysis is looking at principles that are based on the Universal Laws that drive the markets, which all revolve around the Law of Supply and Demand.

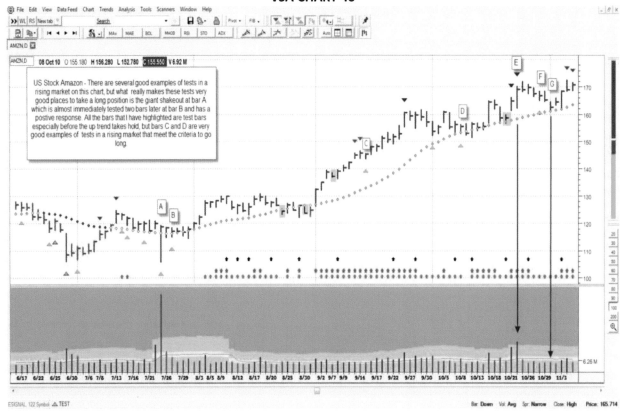

Imbalances of supply and demand are happening all the time, but the effect on price movement will vary greatly between an imbalance of supply and demand seen on a 1 minute time frame and an imbalance of supply and demand seen on a daily or weekly time frame. Obviously, if a principle is observed on a higher time frame like a weekly chart or even a monthly chart, the effect on the price movement is going to be greater.

A *Test in a Rising Market* is at its highest probability when it appears at the bottom of the up-trend channel. It is also high probability if you see a healthy, but not excessive increase in Volume on the up bars that close higher than the preceding bar. Increasing Volume on up bars and decreasing Volume on down bars after the market has seen a serious *Sign of Strength* is very bullish, as observed in **VSA CHART 40**. If you detect ultra high Volume coming in on the up move, this will represent supply entering the market and you should wait to see if *Test* that supply.

Look at **VSA CHART 40.** We see this exact principle at work at bar E where there is an ultra high Volume up bar as supply enters the market. The TradeGuider software will put a red indicator on this bar and the result of this supply appearing is that the stock falls and it will initially *Test* at point F. You will notice that this *Test* fails and will be *Tested* again at point G. Also notice that the Volume at point F and G is very low on these down bars while the stock is in an up-trend. After point G, there will be a successful *Test* and the stock makes the next leg up.

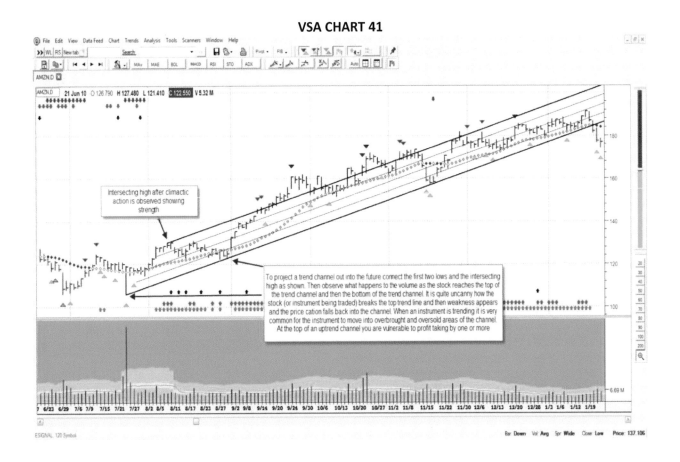

VSA CHART 41 is the same as **VSA CHART 40** of the US stock, Amazon, but this time we have drawn a trend channel from the first point of the *Climactic Shakeout* with the intersecting high and first low after the *Shakeout*. These trend lines are very useful reference points when the stocks or instrument being traded reaches either the top or bottom.

At the bottom, look for *Tests, No Supply, Reversal Bars,* or *Strength Coming In*. Again, it is important to reiterate that strength comes in on down bars, which is when price closes lower than the preceding bar. This is because the Smart Money will buy at lower price levels and sell at higher price levels. This is why strength appears on down bars and weakness appears on up bars.

In summary, when you go long after observing a *Test*, it must be confirmed that it is in the right place. This is very much the same when *No Supply* is detected. You should see suggestions of strength on a *Climactic Action* bar in the background. This will often be a *Shakeout* or *Selling Climax*. The result of this is a clear up-trend forming after the *Climactic Selling* has taken place.

When I indicate that you should look at the background in your analysis, you need to be somewhat subjective. You will see in **VSA CHART 40** that the *Climactic Shakeout* at bar A is actually around 70 bars back from the right edge of the chart.

I have observed charts where the *Climactic Selling* has had an effect on the price movement for over 400 bars and there are other charts where the market has an opposing principle within a short period of time, for example, 100 bars.

At this point, you will see extremely high *Climactic Selling* as the Smart Money buy when the price falls. After the supply is removed, the trend begins to move up. Then you see an equally ultra high Volume bar, but this time, it is a *Buying Climax* and the Smart Money players are now actively selling what they bought before, at lower prices.

Always pay attention to the last highest Volume bar in your largest time frame since it will have the greater effect on price movement. The markets will always move up, down, and sideways, so there are always opportunities to buy and sell.

You want to be able to recognize the higher probability opportunities. Next I would want to observe background information on a chart. **I am looking for the highest Volume bars I can find, either on the downside if I am looking to go long or to the upside if I am looking to short.** After that, I want to see confirmation of the strength or weakness. VSA is not just about analyzing one bar, or just one time frame- it is about looking at the bigger picture and breaking down your analysis into the time frames that suit your personal trading strategy and lifestyle.

VSA CHART 42

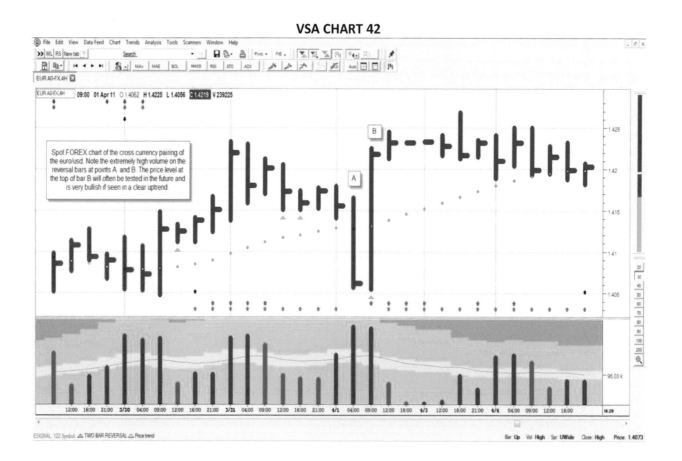

Reversal Bars and Bottom Reversals

This VSA indication of strength analyzes two bars. The *Two Bar Reversal* could also be described as a *Two Bar Shakeout* because they both have the same effect.

Bar A is marked down on very high or ultra high Volume and closes on the low, often at previous support levels as observed in **VSA CHART 42.** Bar B completely reverses and closes above bar A. Even if bar B closes level it is still a strong *Sign of Strength*. Due to the ultra high Volume at bar B, you will often see the market move up a little and then sideways before price action comes down into the body of bar B. Once there, it will *Test* the very high or ultra high Volume on bars A and B.

Bottom Reversals take after a down-trend has been in place and will often cause a change in trend. Frequently, you will see in that in smaller time frames *Bottom Reversals* will appear, but in the larger time frames are actually translated as a *Shakeout* on one bar. In the smaller time frame, such as a 60 minute price bar, when the *Shakeout* begins, the price is marked down heavily on high Volume. Over the next few hours, the hourly price bars show the mark down and the mark back up, but when observed on a 4 hour bar, or even the daily chart, for example, you will see all this activity on one bar as a *Climactic bar*. That is why the smaller time frames often lead to the bigger picture when it appears.

If you see unusual Volume coming in on the smaller time frames, the VSA principles may appear as *Reversal Bars* or *Strength Coming In*, when in fact, the larger time frame may show a *Shakeout*, or a similar principle.

When deciding to go long after seeing a *Reversal Over Two Bars* or a *Bottom Reversal,* keep in mind the following:

- If the Volume on bar B is ultra high, the market is very likely to come back and *Test* that area again. Often, this will begin an up-trend if seen after a *Bottom Reversal,* or it will be the start of the next leg up, if seen during an existing up-trend.

- Draw a line above the top of bar B and wait for price action to penetrate that line. Then look for a *Test* of that price area. It is a safer entry.

- If you are in an up-trend and you see a *Reversal* followed by a *Test* or *No Supply,* this is very bullish.

- If you have seen a down-trend and you observe a *Bottom Reversal*, especially if the Volume is ultra high, this area will often need a *Test* in the future. If you go long, beware of the possibility of another *Test* and manage your position accordingly.

Remember that *Reversal bars* are actually *Shakeouts over two bars*.

Why is the Smart Money shaking the market out?

It is because they want higher prices. In order to do this, they hunt down stops, as observed at bar A in **VSA CHART 42**. On this chart, they actually mark down to a prior support level almost to the tick. I see this very often when trading the forex and currency futures markets. *Reversal bars*, like many VSA *Signs of Strength*, are bullish when confirmed, although, I have seen many *Reversals* and the market has not even waited for the *Test,* acting like a *Shakeout.*

Be aggressive. Buy the top of the *Reversal* at bar B, or be conservative and wait for the *Test* or *No Supply* with an order above the *Test* or the *No Supply* bar.

Absorption Volume or Pushing Through Supply

If you observe an *Old Point of Supply* to the left hand side with very high or ultra high Volume at the price level to the left of the chart with the market re-approaching that level, then, as we have seen in the earlier example of the US stock, JP Morgan, that stock or instrument will often get *Gapped Up* on ultra high Volume at these levels. The motive is to trap unwary traders and investors that are ignorantly buying these tops. We saw that result on the JP Morgan charts as they collapsed.

Often, however, there are two VSA principles are seen as a bull market is developing or underway. These principles are called *Absorption Volume* and *Pushing through Supply*. If a market has previous areas of supply that caused resistance by overcoming demand, in order to move through this old area, it will need effort.

Remember that one of the laws that drive the market is *Effort versus Result*. If we see high or ultra high Volume pushing through this resistance level, followed by the next few bars showing *No Demand* evidenced by falling prices, we can see and conclude that there has been *No Result from Effort*. This is a strongly bearish indication that will cause the market to fall, or at the very least, move sideways.

If, however, the Smart Money is bullish and want higher prices, they will be prepared to absorb the sellers who have been locked in at price levels that the market is now re-approaching. As the market pushes through this old price level on high Volume, look for evidence that this is now the Smart Money absorbing the supply. They will have the expectation to mark the price up further without causing the previous weak holders to sell, since they are now seeing rising prices.

For this supply to be absorbed, the Smart Money will almost immediately, or at least within 10 bars, *Test* the market to flush out any sellers. Also, if the Volume is very low on the *Test* and the next bar is up, this is confirmation that the very high Volume on bar A is absorbing the supply, so it is, in fact, bullish.

This is rarely seen in bearish markets and is much more frequent in bullish markets. The trend builds up from some type of *Climactic Action* on the down bars in a price action area where the Smart Money professionals have been actively accumulating.

On **VSA CHART 43**, we can clearly see this principle. At points A, B, and C, we observe prior resistance to higher prices despite three attempts to rally on ultra high Volume. At point D, we re-approach the same price level and see a surge in Volume on an up bar closing near the prior resistance level. The black line drawn at the bottom of bar D is very important.

US Stock PALM - Weekly Chart
We note the resistance at points A, B and C and there is no result from the effort on bar C. The stock re approaches this area at point D and the volume is ultra high. We would expect to see a negative reaction to price after seeing such high volume so we let the following bars tell us the true picture. If bar D was seriously weak then I wait for the low of the bar to be penetrated by price action and then go up on No Demand for confirmation but that does not happen in this example. Bars E and F are the real clues here. F being a test that ended the day a slight up bar, but a great test when we look at the volume. This is confirmation of a breakout and higher prices to come.

The stock price does not penetrate the low of bar D so that is a good place to put a stop if you are buying on the tests at E and F.

CHART VSA 43 shows the weakness at bar D caused a serious fall in prices. You would expect the price to penetrate this level and then confirm the weakness by going back up to the black line marked on *No Demand*.

However, what we see is the opposite *Signs of Strength* appearing and *Testing*. This is a very important principle because many traders who are first introduced to VSA will assume that every ultra high Volume up bar is a *Sign of Weakness* and that the market will then fall. Traders I have met that utilize these VSA principles say that they short nearly all the ultra high Volume up bars, some with greater success than others.

The price falls after bar D has formed. However, we subsequently see in this example, what is known as a *countermanding* indicator. After what looks like a serious *Sign of Weakness* at bar D, the stock is not behaving with lots of weak bars as expected. In fact, it is quite the contrary.

After this weakness you would expect to see *Up-thrusts, No Demand* bars, and further, *Supply Coming In*, but we actually get *Stopping Volume* and *Tests*. Also note that if using the TradeGuider trending system, we never change to red bars and red diamonds, proof that this weakness did not change the trend.

In the next chapter, we will examine how to create a VSA trading plan now that you have become familiar with the overall concept of strength and weakness revealing itself in the Volume, the Spread, and Closing Price of the bar.

CHAPTER 8
Developing a Personal Trading Plan Using Volume Spread Analysis

Fail to plan – plan to fail. Trading is a business. It just might be the biggest business on the planet. Millions of dollars exchange hands each trading day in the various financial markets across the world. Where there is money to be made, you can be sure there are professional operators at work- the Smart Money.

It is easy to access the financial markets. There are low commission costs and the markets are accessible to anyone with a computer, an internet connection, and a brokerage account. With those conditions, it is no surprise that there are many amateur and junior traders who do not know what they are getting in to.

I have conducted many seminars and webinars in several countries around the globe, which has allowed me the opportunity to speak to and meet with many retail traders and investors of all experience levels. One of the most striking things I have found is the vast majority of retail traders and investors have absolutely no trading plan, and at worst, they are not trading the markets at all, they are gambling!

Most have been looking for the Holy Grail of trading, or a system that will always be right and continually churn out profit after profit. They spend thousands, or even hundreds of thousands of dollars in search of this miraculous financial 'system' that will make them millions overnight.

Good luck with your search if you are one of those traders or investors that are hunting for that magic bullet! You may be looking for a very long time and waste a whole lot of money before finding it.

Are there computerized systems in the markets today that have certain programmed systems that use 'high frequency trading techniques' to gain an edge in the market?

Yes, there most certainly are, but you will rarely hear anything about them. Attention was recently drawn to the use of computerized trading with the potential of moving markets on a grand scale. In 2009, Sergey Aleynikov, a Russian programmer, was accused of stealing computer code from, Goldman Sachs, a large institutional bank in the United States. The code was apparently capable of potentially large-scale market manipulation, or "sophisticated, high-speed and high-volume trades on various stock and commodity markets", as described by Goldman.

My personal opinion is that this was what actually caused the May 6th Flash Crash. Of course, it's only an opinion and there is no hard evidence as to what precisely happened. However, the other explanations made publicly at the time did not seem credible and there were many subsequent explanations that didn't seem to make any sense at all.

VSA is a discretionary system and requires you to use some common sense rules and observations, as well as developing your own individual skill as trader or investor. Just like playing a sport, you must practice to become a professional. You need to plan your goals, have a strategy, and then practice, practice and practice! In order to get on the right track from day one when using Volume Spread Analysis, you'll need to 'unlearn' any bad habits you may have picked up in the past.

The story of UK fund manager, Philip Friston, is a great example of this. Philip's story will be of great comfort to those of you still struggling to be consistent and profitable. His interview in the following chapter is very revealing and will relieve the bewilderment you may have when learning to be a consistent and successful trader or investor using VSA.

The first thing to look at when developing your plan is, in fact, yourself. You need to look inwards at what makes you tick, what drives you, and what type of personality you are. Even if you don't like the answer, it is most important to ask yourself, "Can I afford to lose most or all of my risk capital trading the markets without affecting my current lifestyle or having to move my retirement?"

If you answered "No", then you should think about your options carefully and consult a qualified financial adviser before making a decision to trade. If you answered "Yes", then you are in a good place to develop your plan and begin the task of learning to trade and invest in the markets using Volume Spread Analysis.

Also, always keep in mind that whenever you are in the market, your money is at risk. We will talk a bit about managing risk later on. Among the great traders, fund managers, and investors I have met, all of them have a great understanding of risk versus reward and when to exit a losing trade.

You must do a self-analysis and ask yourself the additional upcoming questions. I suggest you write down the answers and start to decide which markets you would like to trade. Following are some questions you need to answer to ascertain what is best for you:

- Do I currently have another job, full-time or part-time, that requires my attention?

- How much time can I dedicate to my analysis and trading each week?

- Am I going to trade longer-term positions using End-of-Day charts or am I going to trade during the intraday hours when the markets are open?

- Am I going to be conservative or aggressive in my trading or investing?

- Do I have difficulty being patient, or perhaps, do I have attention deficit disorder? Many losing traders I have met admit that A.D.D. is their worst enemy, but this can be managed.

- Do I understand the nature of risk?

- Do I currently have a system or have I committed to learning a system, such as Volume Spread Analysis?

- If yes, do I *believe* in the system I am using to make my trading and investing decisions? I feel that this is actually one of the most important questions. I will cover more on belief in Chapter 9.

- Do I understand the differences between trading instruments such as futures, options, stocks, forex etc.?

- Do I know the tick value for the instrument I am going to trade? For instance, the E-mini S&P futures contract traded on the CME Group has a $12.50 value for each quarter point tick, which means one point is $50.00 for one contract traded.

- Do I have a broker that I can trust and who can give me good advice? If you are new to trading the markets, having a great broker is vital.

To assist you, the above questionnaire can also be found at www.tradingintheshadow.com along with some suggestions to point you in the right direction. The website has many resources to help you get started using VSA as your analysis methodology, but can also be helpful for more experienced VSA traders.

My good friend, a trading psychologist and VSA expert, Dr. Gary Dayton, created the questionnaire. Gary specializes in helping traders understand what is right for their individual personality types. It will help you identify what resources you may need, as well as provide suggestions as to where to go to get that information.

Which Markets to Trade

Tom Williams chose to make his fortune trading the stock market back in the 1950's and 1960's, but that's because there weren't very many choices of markets to trade. We are fortunate enough to have several to choose from today, but you need to decide which market is best for you.

There are a number of factors that will help you decide what markets to trade. You need to consider how much time you have to determine whether or not you want to take a longer term view of the markets direction or be in and out, quickly trading the live charts intraday. Both trade timing scenarios have advantages for the trader or investor.

Although, I must emphasize that if you are going to use VSA or are already use VSA, *it doesn't matter which market or which time frame you use.*

Depending on what Volume Spread Analysis is telling me, I personally like to trade futures and forex intraday, or stocks and commodities swing trading positions, which can hold for weeks and months.

Remember there are many countries that have different rules and regulations. Make sure to check your own country of residence in regard to legislation applicable to your financial trading activities.

For example, many countries have their own index made up of stocks within an index with regulations set by that index's country. For example, if you are in Malaysia, you cannot short a stock because it is against regulations. If you are very new to trading and investing, I can suggest two quick and easy ways to learn the core VSA principles prior to developing your trading plan:

- First, invest in the longer term in the stock market analyzing daily and weekly charts while you learn the principles.

- Secondly, if using the TradeGuider software, use the scanner for stocks or commodities so you can see which ones are undergoing Smart Money buying or selling.

As Tom Williams taught me, he learned to follow a few essential rules developed by Richard Wyckoff. The TradeGuider program-coded scanner is based on those same principles created by Wyckoff from over 100 years ago. Tom often jokes that if Wyckoff had the computer technology back then, he would have done what Tom did and program the principles into a software system! That is why I believe Wyckoff, Williams, and I are connected in some way. We have the same desire and passion to educate the uninformed trading public!

Richard Wyckoff taught us to trade stocks that are acting in harmony with the parent index they are in. His rules are simple, but critical. If trading the stock market, it is obvious to have stocks be part of your trading plan. Wyckoff's strategy and other points to consider when buying or selling stocks:

- Wyckoff studied market action based on Volume and price analysis.

- Wyckoff determined where risk and reward were optimal for trading.

- Wyckoff studied the psychology of trading and why the Smart Money will buy and sell only at a certain times. Wyckoff coined the term *Composite Operator*, which is a synonym for the Smart Money. He would simply measure the activity, or the Volume, on the ticker tape, which reflected the consensus of the trading opinion amongst the big hitters.

- Confirm the trend and position within the trend of the market you are analyzing.

- Select stocks that are in harmony with the market direction. Bull market: stronger. Bear market: weaker.

- Identify stocks that have built a 'cause' for a move up or down.

- Determine the stocks readiness to move. Many Wyckoffians use Point and Figure charts to look for the nine buying and selling tests.

- Time your entry when there is a turn in the general market using the three laws that govern all financial market behavior:

  ✓ Supply Versus Demand
  ✓ Cause Versus Effect
  ✓ Effort Versus Result

If you follow these rules, become contrarian in your thinking, and study the VSA principles closely, in no time, you will start to read the chart just like a professional trader and investor. It is very possible to achieve great success if you are prepared to put in a little effort.

I started my trading career trading the United States futures and forex markets and opened a demo trading account. It was beneficial because I was able to practice trading in live market conditions before funding a real account. Luckily, I had no 'baggage', bad habits, or useless analysis techniques since I never had experience of trading the markets before, and I was also very fortunate to be surrounded by great traders and VSA experts that were able and willing to teach me first hand.

That's how I did it. I opened an account with Infinity Futures (www.infinityfutures.com), a highly respected and reputable futures brokerage firm in Chicago. I was able to download their highly acclaimed Infinity AT charting platform and order execution DOM (depth of market). I then immediately started taking practice trades using a simulated account, not real money, in order to refine my trade set-ups.

Things have progressed further today and Infinity now offers free charting software for 30 days, with the ability to add in the TradeGuider VSA Studies and Trending systems for a small ongoing monthly fee. You can also get similar charts using eSignal, and another brokerage firm I have an account with and also recommend is PFG Best (www.pfgbest.com).

If you do not want to be overwhelmed, I suggest using VSA for End-of-Day analysis (EOD). Stocks are a great place to start. The VSA principles are applicable to trading intraday and can be successfully learned using the longer term time frames. Also, the data is very inexpensive. TradeGuider Systems International is partnered with Thomson Reuters, which they will provide you with two months of free data if you are a new TradeGuider End-of-Day software user (visit www.tradeguider.com for details).

In my first days learning how to trade, I developed a plan that has served me well ever since, and it could act as a guide for you to start your individual plan. As Tom taught me, remember, each market has a 'personality' of its own. There are specialists and market makers at work, as well as professional traders that have studied their specialty markets for many years.

Tom's syndicate specialized in only twelve stocks, yes that's right, only twelve! In order to be successful, you should concentrate on instruments that are liquid and volatile. Believe it or not, volatility is a trader's best friend! Volatility is created by the Smart Money and their activity gives VSA traders opportunity to trade alongside them.

The instruments that I like to trade are the E-Mini Dow, S&P, and NASDAQ, plus the currency futures contracts, which are all traded on the CME Group, and I trade the forex spot price markets, as well. I chose these instruments because order execution and management is simple to understand and you can trade these markets 24 hours a day- although, I only trade the currency futures after normal market hours.

Many of you reading this book will already be trading and investing, but for those of you who are just beginning, download a demonstration platform and start looking at charts- that is where your journey will begin!

Now we will look at the trading plan in more detail.

Selecting Multiple Time Frames for Your Charts

The markets move tick-by-tick, second-by-second, minute-by-minute, hour-by-hour, day-by-day, week-by-week, and so on.

Wyckoff said, "Tape reading seems to us: the science of determining from the tape the immediate trend of prices. It is a method of forecasting from what appears on the tape now, to what is likely to appear in the future... Thousands of those who operate in the markets now recognize the fact that the market momentarily indicates its own immediate future and that these indications are accurately recorded in the market transactions second-by-second. Therefore, those who can interpret what transactions take place, second-by-second or moment-by-moment, have a distinct advantage over the general trading public."

Wyckoff is telling us that the markets are an unfolding story. If one can interpret the data correctly using the ticker tape, or read the Volume and price action, then the trader or investor that has the proper training can have a distinct advantage over the general trading public, or the Herd.

It is extraordinary that all the same principles seen on a 1 minute chart will work just as effectively on a daily or weekly chart.

VSA CHART 44a and **VSA CHART 44b** show the same principle, but this time, however, it is on a 1 minute chart of the E-mini S&P contract traded on the CME Group.

Point G is actually my favorite set-up, but Tom taught me to be cautious. Note the two points of heavy accumulation at point A and B, which is why you must be cautious buying at bar A. That is why I wait for the change in trend. Bars B and C were shorts that were in harmony with the trend. I have demonstrated that these same principles work in all time frames, but you must decide which time frames are best to use.

VSA CHART 44a

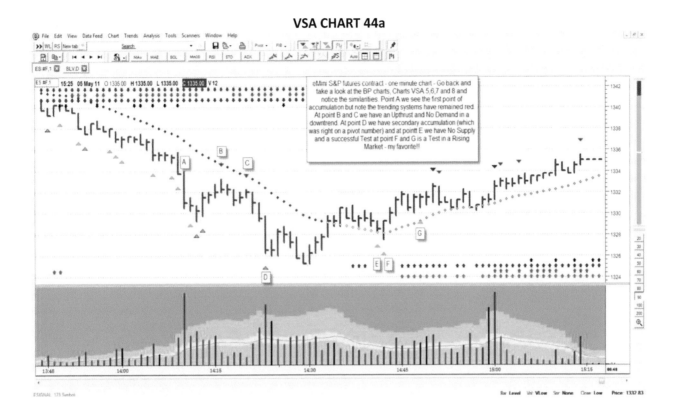

You can choose any time frame that best suits your personality and trading style. That is the wonderful thing about VSA! It works for scalping the market, as well as for investing in the market. It is dangerous to assume that there is a one-style-fits-all trading method. That approach does not exist and the snake oil salesmen in our industry rely on the suckers who believe it does! Traders and investors are bombarded with false advertisements promising a guaranteed technique to make you a successful trader or investor. 99.99% of the products advertised are crap!

If you have been unfortunate enough to be the victim of these schemes, I am sorry you found out the hard way, but now, at least you know the truth. You can delete all the emails and ignore all the adverts falsely promising quick riches because that's all they are, false promises.

You are the best guide as to what time frames can accommodate you best. You are unique in every way and don't ever forget that! Individuality is our most important asset when we trade, especially when it comes to our own ideas and thoughts that lead to our decisions. Choosing the time frames that suited for you will be a trial and error process, but that is why I highly recommend that you first try out a simulated trading account (you can find some to download for free at www.tradingintheshadow.com).

For each market, I find there are different time frames that are more effective than others.

End-of-Day Time Frames for Stocks, Commodities, etc.

- Use the highest time frame to start your analysis

- Monthly chart with 120 bars or 10 years of data: Look for prior areas of support and resistance that have ultra high Volume (see **VSA CHART 9**). These will be able to help you identify *Trigger Numbers* where the Smart Money will show their hands

- Weekly chart with 360 bars

- Daily chart with 1,080 bars

- Swing traders can also use a 240 minute (4H) chart and a 60 minute (1 H) chart to spot early signs of heavy distribution or heavy accumulation (eSignal now provides delayed data for a fraction of the cost of Real-Time Data so you can look at smaller time frames in the TradeGuider RT software).

Intraday Time Frames for Futures

- Use the highest time frame to start your analysis

- Daily chart with 500 bars: Use trend channels drawn in place with unusual Volume activity from past bars projected out to the right edge of chart using a horizontal line placed at bottom, top and close of bar. If price approaches these areas during an intraday session, these areas will act as strong support and resistance levels or *Trigger Numbers*.

- 30 minute chart: Use trend lines in place and pivot numbers added. TradeGuider has a proprietary way of calculating these numbers based on our specific formula, but standard pivots applied are fine as well.

- 15 minute chart: Look for confluence of trend with a 5 minute chart or unusually high or low Volume.

- 5 minute chart: Execute trades from this time frame in a fast moving market and confirm when you go down to a 3 minute chart.

Scalping

- For scalping the market, 1 minute charts are fine, but should be used with at least a 3 minute and 5 minute chart, as well. Even scalpers should pay attention to the daily chart to find *Trigger Numbers* so you can forecast where your highest probability trades will come from.

Intraday Time Frames for Stock Trading

- Use the highest time frame to start your analysis.

- Weekly chart with 360 bars: Use a trend channel drawn in place and unusual Volume activity from past bars projected out to right edge of chart using horizontal line placed at bottom, top and close of bar. If price approaches these areas during intraday session these areas will act as strong support and resistance, or *Trigger Numbers.*

- Daily chart with 1,080 bars: Look for any unusual Volume bars and draw a horizontal line that projects out the top, bottom, and close of the bar. If price action approaches these areas during intraday trading then these areas will act as strong support or resistance. Remember when projecting these lines out you only need to do this when you can clearly see that price action at the right edge of the chart is approaching these old levels, you do not need to go back and do this for every ultra high or ultra low Volume bar.

- 240 minute (4H) chart: Use a trend channel to find the last active short-term trend. If the daily trend lines up with the 240 minute (4H) trend and the 60 minute lines up as well, then any trade taken against this common trend is very risky.

- 60 minute chart: Use a trend channel and look for a confluence in trends.

- 15 minute chart: Look for early signs of unusual Volume.

- 5 minute chart: Execute trades from this time frame. In a fast moving market, go down to a 3 minute chart to confirm.

Please note that if you are using the TradeGuider EOD software system, it is prudent to do a stock scan and indicator scan at the end of each week to identify stocks that are acting stronger or weaker than the parent index, as well as to find stocks that have Climactic Action signals at the right edge of the chart. This will help you considerably narrow down which stocks to trade intraday because these will be the stocks that will move fast.

Time Frames for Spot Forex

It is now possible to get daily Volume for forex, but how can Volume be relevant for spot forex when there is no centralized exchange?

I want to show you something very powerful. Even if you are not a forex trader, it is relevant to everyone and any one that trades or invests. What I will show you will definitely prove that Volume is activity and it will become apparent when the Smart Money is active because they leave behind such obvious foot prints.

I will first explain why we are able to accurately analyze Volume in the spot forex market. In my trading, I use eSignal to get data for the TradeGuider software, but Tick Volume data is now widely available from many other brokerage firms and data providers. Many people assume there is no Volume in forex, but eSignal, including the large number of other data providers, produce a Volume histogram with their own forex data. Here is an excerpt from our forex fact sheet available at www.tradeguider.com:

Q: Where does eSignal get their forex data?
Forex data is from GTIS, an affiliate of FT Interactive Data, sister company to eSignal and the primary supplier of foreign exchange information used by traders, corporations, and financial institutions for over 20 years. They provide spot rates for more than 100 currencies, as well as precious metals, cross rates, and forward rates with nearly 200 global bank and broker contributions in Asia/Pacific Rim, Russia, Europe, and North America.

Additional contributors consist of Garban Intercapital, the world's leading derivatives, securities, and money broking business, as well as Tullett & Tokyo Liberty, one of the largest inter-dealer brokers in the world. Forex Market Depth has the ability to view the best bid/ask by forex contributor. Foreign Currency Options (FCO) from the Philadelphia Stock Exchange (PHLX) is the first organized stock exchange in the US and one of North America's primary marketplaces.

Q: I'm seeing the Volume histogram update on Forex issues in eSignal, what does that Volume represent?

The Volume histogram for forex represents the number of transactions or ticks- not true trade size activity. It is much like most futures contracts, where the Volume histogram reflects the Volume of transactions or updates during each given interval. **It is important to understand that TradeGuider does not need actual Volume, but relative Volume compared to the previous bar to produce a VSA indicator.** The Volume in forex markets can be seen as activity- it is this activity that TradeGuider picks up extremely well when using Tick Volume.

Tom Williams, the creator of TradeGuider and the Volume Spread Analysis methodology answers the question of, 'How do the VSA principles work in Spot Forex and TradeGuider?':

First of all, you have to realize that the Smart Money, or professional money, is very active in the forex market. The professional money are also known as the trading syndicates, large institutional banks, individual traders with huge capital, other large financial institutions, or certain hedge funds, such as The Quantum Fund operated by George Soros." (You can get more information by visiting www.financialpolicy.org)

These affluent individuals and wealthy organizations are very secret in their dealings. They do not want others to know their movements. Seeing the lack of Volume is the result of this. **However, Tick Volume works.** *Tick Volume is added to the price movement on every price tick, either up or down. One trader may deal in 5M, while the very next trader only deals 500K, but we get one tick each dealer.*

Bear in mind that from the Tick Volume created, 90% will be from the Smart Money and their dealers.

When these very large orders go through, they have a following. It is the same as the futures pits. This activity automatically creates more ticks, which means higher Volume. TradeGuider will analyze the Tick Volume as if it were real Volume. This will clearly show the Smart Money participating, or just as importantly, not participating in the movement of a currency. When we hear of strength and weakness in a currency, this is nothing more than professional support, or lack of it, and it you can clearly see it on a TradeGuider chart.

Remember in 1992 when George Soros massively shorted the British Pound, forcing The Bank of England to eventually withdraw from the European Exchange Rate Mechanism? This is just one very well-known example of the Smart Money having a dramatic effect on a currency, but this happens every day. Fortunately, the enlightened traders that are aware of what is really going on in the markets are able to see it. If you have the knowledge and know exactly what to look for, you will be able to recognize the Smart Money trying to make their secretive moves against the Herd.

Have a look at the chart and notice the Volume during that famous move by George Soros.

GEORGE SOROS CHART

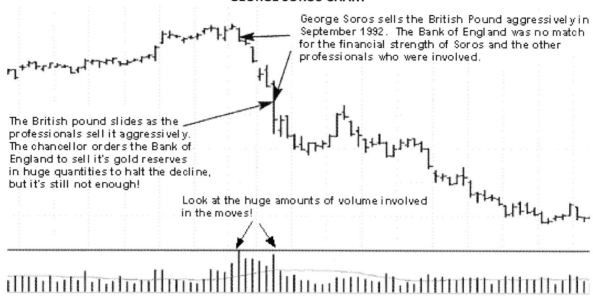

George Soros sells the British Pound aggressively in September 1992. The Bank of England was no match for the financial strength of Soros and the other professionals who were involved.

The British pound slides as the professionals sell it aggressively. The chancellor orders the Bank of England to sell it's gold reserves in huge quantities to halt the decline, but it's still not enough!

Look at the huge amounts of volume involved in the moves!

So in 1992, the British pound fell so sharply that Britain was forced to leave the Exchange Rate Mechanism (ERM). What do you think was behind this famous fall? Yes, you guessed it, Professional Money! The Smart Money in question was the Quantum Fund, which was run by the renowned speculator, George Soros.

He and his analysts had spotted a potential weakness in the ERM. During the weeks before the massive sell-off of the British pound, George Soros was busy exchanging seven billion US Dollars for German Deutsche Mark!

When the time was right, he moved in fast and sold the British Pound. As the Pound fell, the Deutsche Mark rose, creating huge profits for Soros. As soon as the news reached the other professionals, they followed suit.

The onslaught was too overwhelming for Norman Lamont, the UK Chancellor of the Exchequer during that time. In an attempt to halt the slide, Lamont resorted to selling some of Britain's gold reserves. He raised interest rates three times in one day, but this was still no match for the professionals!

Tick Volume is as valuable as exchange traded Volume in VSA. **VSA is analyzing Volume *relative* to the Volume bars preceding the live bar when it has filled.**

What do I mean by 'relative'? In the situation of trading the markets, relative means I can compare activity and other factors by simply using my eyes and glancing at a chart. It means I can decipher whether a Volume bar is ultra high or ultra low or see if the Spread of a bar is ultra high or ultra low, just by looking at the last 25 to 50 bars around it.

Let me give an analogy of a similar situation. Many of you regularly attend my seminars or webinars and are aware that I live right in the heart of downtown Chicago near the financial district.

I was born and raised in the U.K, but while living here in the US and especially in Chicago (does Michael Jordan ring a bell?), I quickly realized that basketball is extremely popular. Due to his skill, but especially his height, one of the most recognized players in the NBA is Yao Ming, a member of the Houston Rockets team.

Yao is one of the tallest players in the NBA, towering at seven foot six inches and well above average height. I am six foot two inches, only slightly above average for a man. These days, the average height of an adult male in the US is between 5'7"- 6'0". So in comparison to the average American man, Yao Ming is considered to be very tall.

Put a group of people in a line-up and include Yao Ming, me, my daughter Olivia who is only 3 feet tall, and a variety of other people of average American male height. If an alien randomly landed before us from outer space and examined this line-up, the alien's observation about the height of a human would be relative to those present.

It would probably look at me and say I am tall and then look at my daughter and say she is super short (ultra short or ultra low), but the alien would then see the others, who are quite similar, but in-between myself and Olivia in height. Then it would observe Yao Ming. It would see Yao Ming is significantly taller (ultra tall or ultra high) than everyone else around him.

When you apply this to Volume on the bottom of your chart and you observe ultra high Volume comparable to Yao Ming, and just as importantly, very low Volume as represented by my daughter Olivia, both are very significant on a chart.

High Volume is the Smart Money activity and low Volume is Smart Money inactivity.

Let me now prove once again that Volume is extremely valuable to you as a forex trader. If you are one of those trading without Volume, you are trading in the dark!

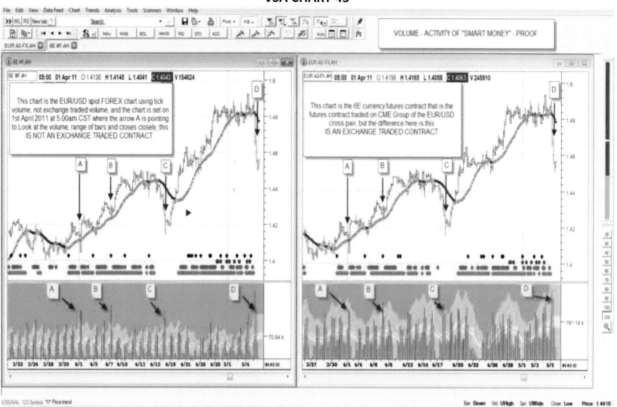

Examine the chart on the right of **VSA CHART 45**, which is a split screen. It is a chart of the 6E currency futures contract, which is the cross currency pair of the EURO/USD traded on the CME Group. The chart on the left of **VSA CHART 45** is a spot forex contract that is not traded on any exchange. In this case, I can only use the Tick Volume (activity Volume) I am receiving from eSignal.

If we examine the Volume at points A, B, C, and D, which is marked in yellow post-it boxes with red arrows, compare it to the Spread and the Closing Price of the bars at points A, B, C, and D marked with the white boxes and black arrows. You will observe that the two charts, apart from looking very close in shape, both have the ultra high Volume at almost exactly the same place and time. Not only that, all of the points, A, B, C and D the Volume, price Spread and the Closing Prices are almost identical. How can this be?

The chart on the left shows exchange-traded Volume coming from the CME Group and the chart on the right shows Tick Volume from eSignal. I have deliberately switched off the VSA indicators to make the charts more visible, but the VSA indicators are almost identical. Even though the data comes from different sources, you will not always get the exact identical indicators, although, many will have the same numbers.

I have read numerous misleading articles and threads in forums (such as www.forexfactory.com), which suggest that Volume is unusable in analyzing spot forex. That statement is far from the truth and very misleading. At times, Tom and I have been convinced that misinformation is being posted into these forums to confuse the forex traders that are trying to make an honest living by making a consistent profit trading the spot forex market. With that in mind, here are some facts:

- Tick Volume or activity Volume can be used in VSA and Tick Volume is used by many TradeGuider customers.

- When the Smart Money is active, they are active in the cash markets and the futures markets at the same time. Sometimes the future will move a few seconds before the spot or cash market and actually give you an advantage, but that's only if you can read the chart. This applies to the main indices like the S&P, Dow, FTSE, etc.

- If you hear news coming from a large world bank and they advise that they are going to intervene in their currency, look at the chart before you believe them! What they state publicly will most often have the complete opposite effect on the actual price movement. This false news was created to initially to wrong foot the uninformed Herd. Remember, the chart never lies!

- One of our customers, Tim Rayment, won the World Cup Trading Championship while trading real money in a live trading competition, not once, but twice, by trading spot forex. The article from SFO Magazine is located at the end of the book. We re-published this article with kind permission of SFO Magazine and Tim Rayment. TradeGuider would like to give a special thanks to Tim Rayment for being gracious to acknowledge Tom Williams and TradeGuider.

Now we will look at time frames are optimal for trading the spot forex markets, regardless of which pair you are trading, starting with the larger time frame first:

- 240 minute chart with trend channel and 500 bars to see the overall major trend.

- 60 minute chart with trend channel to find the last active short-term trend. If the 240 minute trend lines up with the 60 minute and the 15 minute trend, then any trade taken against this trend is considered very risky.

- 15 minute chart with trend channel and *Trigger Numbers* going back up to 500 bars (but 200 bars is often adequate) look for early signs of unusual Volume. This is the chart I would usually execute trades from.

- 5 minute chart: Execute trades from this time frame in a fast moving market only.

The key to using all these time frames in unison is to find moments when at least 75% of those time frames are in the same trend.

For example, if the 5, 15, and 60 minute chart trends are moving up and the 240 minute chart trend is still trending down, then you want to look for trades to the long side. Make sure you keep in mind that it is very likely that in a downtrend in the higher time frames, as well as what you observe in the smaller time frames may be the beginning of a Volume spike or ultra high Volume bar.

This will obviously show itself in the smaller time frames as prices go up because the Smart Money will sell into the rising price in an overall down-trend, and obviously this will be the complete opposite in an up-trend. The Smart Money buy into a falling price, which is why if the biggest trend is an up-trend in say, the 240 minute time frame, then you will get shorting opportunities in the smaller time frames as the price falls to a level where Smart Money want to accumulate or re-accumulate.

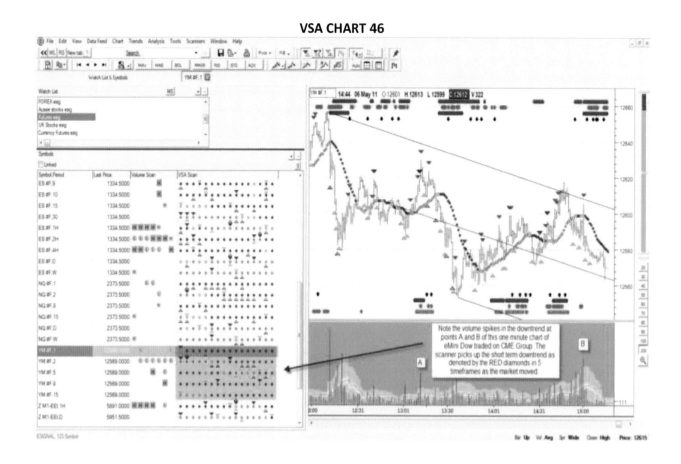

Note the volume spikes in the downtrend at points A and B of this one minute chart of eMini Dow traded on CME Group. The scanner picks up the short term downtrend as denoted by the RED diamonds in 5 timeframes as the market moved.

If all trends are the same in all time frames that you are trading, then this is the perfect moment to trade. The scanner built into TradeGuider Version 4 you can easily and quickly see when that is happening in the live markets and can scan multiple charts in multiple time frames. Please see the example of this at work by looking at **VSA CHART 46,** an E-mini Dow 1 minute chart in a downtrend on 5 time frames. This will show great short trade set-ups when we see the Volume spikes at point A and point B.

Practice, Practice, Practice

The majority of traders and investors I talk to say they just want to get into the live market. They want to experience the thrill of knowing their hard-earned cash is now at risk. Their adrenalin pumps because they know that if they're right, it's going to be a profitable trade. If they're wrong, it is back to the drawing board with losses and often a blown out account. As it has been said, practice makes perfect, and whilst practice will probably never make any trader absolutely perfect, without practicing you have no way of developing a strategy to win!

How did Michael Jordan, Tiger Woods, David Beckham, LeBron James, Michael Schumacher, just to name a few, get to the top of their game? They practiced, practiced, and practiced, until it was second nature to them to be the best of the best.

If you want to trade and invest against some of the most experienced, intelligent, and predatory traders and investors in the world, you better know the game you are getting into. You better practice so that you can hone your skills to you know exactly when to get in to a position, when to get out, or when to let a position ride.

In Tom's book, *"Master the Markets"*, he describes how soldiers train for battle so they can perfect their skills to act automatically in the heat of the battle without needing to think at all. Recently, it had been announced that Osama Bin Laden was shot and killed by a team of highly trained Navy Seals from the United States. There was program on television where a former Seal was interviewed and he described the rigorous training that is required to be a Seal. He specified how thoroughly planned an operation must be in order to be successful, as well as how often and scrupulous the practice and preparation was right before the operation was launched.

When I was creating my own VSA trading plan, it only took me a few weeks to get it right. I suggest you look at the following steps I took during my procedure to developing my own personal trading plan:

- Make sure you are fully familiar with all of the VSA principles.

- Decide which market or markets to trade. I suggest pick one market at a time so you don't get off track.

- Decide which time frames you are going to use, and remember, these can be refined or changed as the plan evolves.

- Select a broker that offers a simulated or demonstration trading platform with a paper trading account that does not require a funds upfront. Most brokers will give a one month trial to their platforms, regardless of which markets you have decided to trade. For example, Infinity Futures brokerage firm has partnered up with TradeGuider Systems and offers a simulated trading platform free for one month and they will also include charts at no charge, as well.

- You will get to decide how much virtual money is in the account, but do not just place trades with no logic or risk reward. For example, imagine you have a $25,000 paper trading account. The first thing you must determine is what your acceptable level of risk will be in any one position. I never risk more than 2.5% of my capital in any position. On a $20,000 account, I will not want to lose any more than $500 if the trade goes wrong. I will close the position or get stopped out. **You must accept that there will be losses when you trade.** Every trader takes losses at some time in their career. Even the very best traders and investors in the world take losses. The key is not to let a position run against you for too long and don't hope and pray that the market will turn back in your favor. Trust me. Hope and prayer will not turn losing trade into a winner, it will only be extreme luck and that is very hard to come by. Just cut your losses and do not let them run so will still have some skin left in the game for the next trade!

- This is next exercise is very important. As you study the charts looking for a trade, write down or verbally record your thoughts and actions in order to archive your behavior for later self-analysis. Describe exactly what you are looking for in that trade set-up, explain what you are actually seeing as you search for it, record how you feel and what you are thinking as the trade is executed, win or lose. After you record these thoughts, go back after the trade has closed and review your decision making process. You will be amazed at what you are really thinking as you scan for trades. You may be pleasantly surprised or you may be horrified. Also, as you enter a trade, take a screenshot of the chart. At the end of the trade, annotate what happened to the trade, like charts in this book are interpreted. It has an educational purpose. When you are able to recognize certain characteristics of bars and patterns, it will all come together. Putting in a little effort will make the learning process much easier. Remember, Effort versus Result is a Universal Law that I apply to the charts, but it also applies to our lives! The more effort, the better the results!

- You must have a risk versus reward ratio before you enter the position. Risk/reward ratios can vary from market to market, but as a simple rule, a 3-1 risk/reward ratio is a good place to start. That means for every dollar you are putting at risk, you are expecting a three-dollar return at a minimum. If your trade set-up does not look like it will give that return, perhaps because it is close to a prior level of support or resistance and you want to take a long trade because the set-up is there, if you can see there is resistance a few ticks above, it best to step aside and wait for the next opportunity.

- As you practice, try different positions for your protective stop. **Always use a stop loss when you trade.** Even if it is only an emergency stop loss that is well away from the price action. An emergency stop loss is there in case of a 'Black Swan' event that can cause the market to crash. You have no guarantee of a fill, but at least you have an order at the exchange that can be triggered. Most retail traders lose consistently because their stops are always getting triggered. Most educators teach the retail trader to use a tight stop loss to prevent excessive losses. I do not suggest that. I would trade a lesser contract size with a wider stop, placing the stop above the last point of supply if you are going short, or at the last point of demand if going long. The last point of supply in a down-trend will appear on an up bar where you see the last ultra high Volume spike in the background. The last point of demand will be where you see a down-bar where the last ultra high Volume spike in an up-trend appears.

- Each week take a few hours to review each chart and each trade. Start putting these in a folder or file that you can call your trading journal. A majority of the most experienced and best traders and investors I have had the privilege to meet still keep trading journals, and rest assured, the Smart Money also track everything they have done in order to review on a constant basis, which is the reason you should do the same.

- Finally, as part of your plan, it is necessary that the place where you make your trading decisions, such as your office or your home office, is conducive to clarity of thought. That place will be different and unique for everyone who reads this book. This too, is very important. In order to make effective trading decisions you must be able to focus and be in 'the zone'. Mark Douglas wrote a great book called, *"Trading in the Zone"*. It describes how to master the markets with a confidence, discipline, a clear mind, and a winning attitude. For one to make good decisions in anything in life we must have some clarity of thought or we give room for mistakes.

So in summary, it is very important to have a plan when you are trading or investing. This plan will allow you to see where you are making good and/or bad trading. The plan will adapt as you learn more and move forward. This can be used as a guideline you can measure against.

Remember, trading is a business. All great businesses have a plan. This isn't just a hobby, or a sport, nor is it gambling against the odds. You have the power and ability to even the odds and be successful as a trader or investor.

The fact that you are at this stage of the book probably means you are ready for the next step.

The power that will ensure you can make money in the markets is the power of belief in your own ability to create abundance and wealth for yourself and others. Using the energy of your thoughts, actions, words, or yourself as a whole, it is possible to have everything you want. It is attainable. I am living proof and have never been happier, despite a few serious setbacks. But from my troubles and strife, I found a very powerful force that can help all traders and investors. In order to learn about this force however, you must open your mind, like I had to. Again, your mind is like a parachute and is best used only when you open it.

In the next chapter, which I believe may be the most important part of the book; I will tell you more about this Power of Belief. This is considered to be the Fourth Universal Law and it can very possibly help you. If you accept this and apply it, this can change your life for the better.

CHAPTER 9
The Power of Belief and the Law of Attraction in Your Trading Strategy

In some ways this will be the most difficult and even most controversial chapter to write, but in other ways, since this topic comes from the heart, it will be the easiest.

Before 2006, I knew little or nothing about the importance of one's own belief system. I had never heard of the Law of Attraction and in fact, I had never even considered that the other Universal Laws, apart from the Law of Gravity, were important to our existence. I was to find out they play a huge part in our everyday lives.

I had an experience in 2006 which led me to information that had a profound effect on my life. While the event itself is irrelevant, what I discovered is extremely important. It was revealed to me that what we think about will have a great effect on what actually happens to us in our lives, the good and the bad. We all have thoughts and that inner 'voice' which talks to us, but have you ever stopped to consider what that voice really is and why it is there? I certainly never did, at least not until 2006. To be quite honest, it meant very little to me- thoughts were simply just 'thoughts' and thoughts could make you feel really good, really bad, and everywhere in between.

So why do I mention the Universal Law of Attraction? Well first, let's look at the origins of the Law of Attraction and its definition.

My opinion of the Universal Law of Attraction is that the universe we inhabit as human beings is made up of energy forces that are only now starting to be understood by mankind.

The Law of Attraction refers to the idea that thoughts influence chance. The Law of Attraction argues that thoughts, both conscious and unconscious, can affect things outside of the head, not just through motivation, but by other means. Simply stated, the Law of Attraction concept is that 'like attracts like'.

Most recently, claims of the Law of Attraction are being supported by a growing body of scientific evidence and opinion. This leads to the conclusion that more research is necessary in regards to this subject in order to enhance our understanding the universe.

In 1910, Wallace Wattles wrote a book called, *"The Science of Getting Rich"*, which was the inspiration for the bestselling book *"The Secret"*, by Rhonda Byrne. *"The Science of Getting Rich"* is one of the books in my recommended reading section listed in www.tradingintheshadow.com. Wallace Wattles stated that "the scientific use of thought consists in forming a clear and distinct mental image of what you want; in holding fast to the purpose to get what you want; and in realizing with grateful faith that you do get what you want".

A consistent theme with Wattles and many other great luminaries of the time is "the insistence that by using our brains and our own thoughts in a harmonious manner with the positive aspects of the universe, we can bring about great and beneficial changes on our lives". Wattles also wrote, "Everything works under the same laws, yesterday, today and forever". He was adamant that we create our own lives. We cannot just sit idly waiting for things to happen.

One of the most fundamental universal rules that we accept as scientific fact began as an Aristotelian hypothesis and then it was rebutted by a more accurate experiment by Galileo. Finally, it would be successfully mathematically postulated and hypothesized by Isaac Newton. As a result, Gravity came to be accepted as a scientifically proven natural law.

We all have the power of producing thoughts and all creative things in human life start from a thought. Ideas manifest in our lives when we take positive action on positive thoughts and unfortunately, the opposite is true as well, with negative action produced by negative.

A manifestation is something that you created. It appears in your life as the result of your thoughts and actions. Many, if not all who read this book will have experienced the feeling of *déjà vu* – that moment in time when you experience a feeling or emotion that makes you feel as though you have been there before. Paying attention to your thoughts and feelings while aware of the power of your ability to create what you want is the key to having an enjoyable and happy life.

In 1912, Charles Haanel wrote *"The Master Key System"*. It provides practical techniques for using the Law of Attraction to manifest love, harmony, happiness, abundance and fulfillment from life. His book inspired further great works from Napoleon Hill, author of *"Think and Grow Rich"* and Ernest Holmes' *"The Science of Mind"*.

The Law of Attraction has been discussed in many books and other writings that go back hundreds of years, but it has recently become more main-stream due to the work of great authors such as Esther and Jerry Hicks, Rhonda Byrne, Michael Lossier, Dr. Joe Vitale, and also Oprah Winfrey, when she featured the subject on her popular daytime talk show.

Like the Universal Law of Gravity, which took from the time of Aristotle till modern day to be scientifically proven, forward thinkers would regard the Law of Attraction as scientifically nascent. Scientists are getting closer and closer to discovering the true power of the human brain, and most importantly, the power of thought.

The common perception even among the professionally trained community is that mind and brain are synonymous. However, in reality, the two entities are separate. The brain, on the one hand, is organically biochemical. The mind is a psychic organ. Seemingly, the riddle to understanding the Law of Attraction lies in understanding the 'glue' that joins both the mind and the body. Science is now beginning to show us that through the process of biochemical generation of electricity in the body, this electrical current joining the body and the mind must be capable of emitting a field of electrical energy which radiates from the body when activated by thought processes.

Just as light has recently been discovered to consist of sub-atomic particles called photons, it is not unreasonable to believe that thoughts could very soon be proven to consist of electromagnetic radiation, a subject to known scientific laws. Such a postulation and hypothesis, if proven, will move the Law of Attraction from the esoteric realm into that of scientifically proven fact. The Law of Attraction would then make sense from such a basis and would be supported by other scientific laws, like synchronicity and resonance, which would explain the idea of 'like attracts like' and other similar concepts.

Take the subject somewhat deeper. The brain consists of four main parts, but for the purposes of this discussion, the largest part that is of interest to us is the cerebrum. The neo cortex of the cerebrum is its surface area and it is in this neo cortex that science tells us that billions of neurons exist there. It is believed that these neurons are constantly sending electrical energy not only to the rest of the cerebrum, but also to other parts of the brain. Therefore by didactic reasoning, neurons are sending energy to other parts of the body.

It is these scientific facts concerning the neuronal electrical activity that gives us a deeper look into comprehending the Law of Attraction when we link it to our current scientific understanding of electro-magnetic radiation and the fields it produces.

The interesting thing is that it is scientifically considered that the cerebrum is the area of the brain where thoughts originate. It is also the place where our abilities to think, read, write, speak, mathematize emerge, as well as the capacity to create things, such as musical compositions and works of art.

More importantly to the subject of the Law of Attraction, the cerebrum is the area responsible for cognitive thoughts, memory, intelligence, and psychic phenomena.

The Law of Attraction seems to be the manifestation of a person using their power of thought and feeling to influence circumstances that have a desirable outcome. By taking action on those positive thoughts and feelings, those desired results can be attained. The opposite is also true. It means that if negative thoughts are developed, and you take action on those ideas, you will have a negative result in your life.

Therefore, on a level of cause and effect, it would seem reasonable to assume that the positive thoughts, or the positive electro-magnetic radiations that we pulsate, would seek to find resonance with similar radiations. When found, the positivity combined will produce the result as a, agreeable outcome. In other words, goal achieved!

Interestingly, the theory of the effect of electromagnetic radiation seems to also have some basis for understanding in the Chaos Theory. The theory argues that tiny local changes in your thoughts can produce larger changes in your circumstances through the electromagnetic radiation of these thoughts to produce, by resonance, the object of your thoughts, which could be either positive or negative.

To try and explain the Chaos Theory, the famous 'Butterfly Effect' suggests that the beating of a butterfly's wings can lead to a hurricane. Supposedly, the minuscule turbulence it generates could predictably lead to a critical combination of air pressure changes, resulting in to a hurricane. Whether that's true or not is yet to be proven, but it is an interesting concept!

The universe is far too vast for the average human being to comprehend or even think about. Even when we start to think about our own lives compared to everything on this planet, we can feel inferior, insecure, and unimportant, but that could not be further from the truth. We are all equally important.
The universe has been created by a higher power, a universal force. This higher being can have a different definition for each individual depending on their upbringing, their country, their religion, and their belief system. Your faith in God or your belief of an existence of a higher power is a choice we all have.

I can only speak from my own experience. I believe that we are all interconnected with that higher power, which I call God. I also believe that we can draw inspiration, ideas, and assistance when we need it, that is, if we are taught how.

If you examine the Chinese philosophy Yin Yang, it is used to describe how polar, contrary forces are interconnected and interdependent in the natural world, yet they give rise to each other in turn. Opposites will therefore only exist in relation to each other. Everything is in perfect balance, which is why we have good and bad things going on in the world at any time.

Unfortunately there is no news in good news. When we watch our televisions or read our newspapers, all we see is bad news and that makes us feel that the world is in a big mess. It simply is not. It is all an intelligent design that has created this, therefore we should work with that intelligence to create better lives for ourselves and those around us.

If we believe that the very base root of our creation consists of our physical bodies charged with electrical and spiritual energy, it makes sense that our thoughts will assist us to connect with the ultimate energy source. The energy that created the universe also created life as we know it.

Imagine that you are a receiver and an emitter of energy. You have states of high energy and states of low energy. Many people who suffer from depression complain of having little or no energy. People who have high energy and make people feel good just by their presence are said to give off a 'good vibe'.

The word vibe refers to vibrational energy and many books have suggested that human beings have different vibrational energy levels that can be attained. This energy will attract similar vibrational levels as the ones they are giving out. It seems 'like would attract like', which brings us round full circle back to the Law of Attraction. The subject is both limitless and interesting, but outside the scope of this book.

So now, why does this theory have a chapter in a book about VSA and chart reading?

Well, when you trade and invest you obviously want to make money. In order to do that, you must first attract money by thinking positively and harmoniously with the universe. This will give you a greater chance of attaining your individual goals, whether it is a financial goal or something else.

You need to set your goals. You then need to focus in on these objectives with clarity and have the expectation of favorable results. Make realistic goals and use the Law of Attraction to get these positive outcomes to manifest in your life. Once you see the power of the Law of Attraction, you will be well on your way to finding true contentment and happiness. If I can do it, you can do it. Anyone can do it.

Hopefully, by sharing my thoughts and research on the subject, it will go a long way in convincing you of the reasonably possible scientific basis of the Law.

The Power of Visualization

In 1999 I had the very fortunate to meet Paul Avins, who is now one of the leading business coaches in the UK (visit his website at www.paul-avins.com for more information). Paul is the one who introduced me to the concept of visualizing success. One day, he suggested we go to a seminar run by Tony Robbins, a well-known and well-respected teacher, author, and speaker in the personal development field (visit www.tonyrobbins.com for more information).

I was extremely skeptical after I paid over $2,000 to find out that part of this seminar required my participation in walking over hot coals shouting out "Cool moss"! Although, I must say, the whole experience was an eye opener for me. I want to thank Tony and Paul for their insights that helped me write this book and decide to cover this subject to help enlighten the reader.

Tony Robbins and Paul Avins explained that to make something positive happen in your life you must take **massive action**. There is a reason out there which explains why human beings hold themselves back in situations. We call this a **self-limiting belief**.

A self-limiting belief often begins with a word or phrase that creates the sentence for the idea you are telling yourself. These words are very common to what traders and investors think as they are about to pull the trigger:

- I cannot
- I will not
- It does not
- I am not sure
- I doubt
- Maybe

- I don't know
- It is impossible
- I am afraid

Positive Belief Systems Result in Positive Manifestations

When I begin my day with positive suggestions and thoughts, miraculous things tend to happen. The feeling of *déjà vu* happened to me in a very strong way back in 2010 at the New York Traders Expo. A few years before, in 2007 I had a very powerful thought. I got the feeling that at in the very near future, I would be trading live, on stage, before a large audience and I would make a winning trade while explaining all the VSA principles at work. As the days passed, I started to play out in my head exactly what I would be wearing, what the trade would look like, and what would happen as I executed that trade. In December of 2009, I received a phone call that would mark the beginning of my powerful thought manifesting into my real life!

These pictures are of me trading live at the New York Trader's Expo at the Trader's Challenge, in 2010. I was able to successfully make a profitable trade when I identified one of my favorite set-ups, a *Test in a Rising Market.*

Having positivity in your thoughts will result in positive outcomes, but know that it does not happen instantly. To be able to think positively on a constant basis comes over time. The more you condition yourself to think this way it will become second nature. Visualize in your mind what you really want. Many practitioners of the Law of Attraction produce a visual board that is made up of pictures and images of what they want in their life. This can be very helpful in focusing your thoughts in a positive direction. Some positive belief statements that go with positive visualization start with:

- I can
- I will
- I am a winner
- It is possible
- Yes
- I am sure
- Definitely
- I am grateful

Overall and in general, the explanations and definitions previously shared is where society stands with the Universal Law of Attraction. At least the part of society that is willing to open their minds and embrace the consequences of such forward thinking.

This chapter is based on an extreme opinion. I say 'opinion' due to the lack of scientific proof of my beliefs, but I feel that will change in the next few years or so. Like the Universal Law of Gravity, it may take several different theorists and a couple of centuries, but there will be a way to measure my happiness, or lack thereof. Know that belief is **vital** if you are trading and investing!

An Inspiring Letter

I would like to acknowledge and thank TradeGuider customer, Rakesh Kumar. He was kind enough to allow me to use his writings from an e-mail he sent me on November 18th, 2005 and I have treasured it ever since. I send it to our customers who are in lack of belief. As you read, I hope this inspires you as it did me:

Hi Gavin,

Once again, I looked at the chart of the week and thought I would bring to your attention a couple of crucial points.

1. Like yesterday, the market was gapped up, trapping and catching all those buy stop losses of those who were shorting overnight. This was followed by a test of our patience to the limit during an extended distribution period. Then bang! Prices were marked down to lock in all the suckers. Look at the moves on DAX, 35-45pts ($800-1000) compared to just a few points on ES-mini. As I said this market is excellent for trading. It would be a good idea to have the last two days analyzed as charts of the week (Buying Climax) by Tom & Sebastian and then archived with the existing one (Selling Climax).

2. Now in the present chart of the week, most would focus on the chart. However, here are a few gems of comments by Tom on "Belief":

- *You have to believe these underlying principles*
- *You have to believe that these markets work on supply and demand.*
- *You have to believe that these markets reflect consensus of professional opinion at that time.*

Also, in his seminars he remarks many times, "If you don't believe me check it out for yourself"
Now hardly anybody pays attention to these words, but I can assure you if you go through the interviews of super traders in Market Wizards, it will be become evident that a total belief in a particular strategy and having the discipline to implement that strategy and accepting the probability of the strategy with every cell in the body, is at the heart of the success of these super traders.

These guys have stuck to simple strategies and their responses have become automatic, there is no conflict in their mindset.

Just like driving, initially we have that fear of accidents coupled with the motivation to learn; hence the anxiety and stress. However, with practice, this conflict is resolved.

Trading which is the most unique profession in the world. Humans are just not hard wired for trading- period (it has to do with dealing with uncertainty continuously).

3. Every trading strategy based around any indicator with over 50% probability would work if a trader totally believed in it and applied it with discipline. However, 90% of the time this will not happen simply because that crucial transformation based on belief has just not happened. So as soon as we are in front of the screen anxiety and conflict sets in. With indicator-based strategy, we don't know "WHY" it is working and that causes conflict, deep down there is that nagging disbelief. Right from birth we have always been seeking answers to "WHY" and this is carried into the trading arena.

4. There is nothing like emotion free trading. The right belief structure has to be in place to resolve the conflict in the mind, uncertainty against total belief in our ability to read the market.

5. This right belief structure can be gained by understanding VSA principles, which governs all the price patterns, price action, and the derivative indicators thereof, i.e. that is the truth of the market. It provides the answer to "WHY" which is what the human mind seeks. Once that is fully accepted into the psyche, the conflict is resolved, emotions can be managed, (e.g. during driving, we still have emotions, we do not drive around like zombies, but we manage them, mind you nowadays this could be argued, with all that evidence of road rage on our streets) trading would then become like driving a Bentley, and this is the only software in the world which allows a trader to achieve that mindset. Mind you sometimes the charts do look cluttered up with all those "H" and diamonds and lines, however as Sebastian says you only need trend lines & Volume and a couple of charts 60min, 15min, 3min to trade effectively.

Excuse the lengthy email but if this helps anybody, it will be most satisfying. Have a look at the attached also.

Best,
Rakesh

-End of letter-

Additionally, here is the body of the attachment from the email:

"Why You Can't Win at Trading (and Only 10% Do)"

What sets the 90% apart from the 10%? Why is one person seemingly able to effortlessly take profits from the market almost on a daily basis and yet another person trading the same market at the same time will be suffering consistent losses?
Already even at this stage the 90% will be thinking that the 10% guys have better indicators or even a Holy Grail trading strategy. On close examination of the 10% however, it will ALWAYS be found that they often use the same software, the same data, the same indicators and often trade at exactly the same time.

If this is the case (and it is) then surely they must be gurus, they must have the 'Midas' touch, the golden key etc.

Well sorry to disappoint you, but once again this is simply not true, the 10% group consists of traders with many years of experience in trading as part of huge organizations and also the one man/woman in his home trading from a simple PC screen. In reality they are a pretty 'ordinary' lot.

They do have one consistent common factor however, which is usually revealed within 5 minutes of meeting them. They are also more often than not the most genuine of people who take a genuine interest in other traders. When one of the 90% meets one of the 10% the very first thing that happens is that the 90% guy wants to find out every technical detail, about every aspect of the 10% guys trading strategy, software etc. In doing this, the real essence of WHY the 10% guy is successful is almost always completely missed.

This happens in much the same way as we miss huge parts of sales talks and yet we still buy the products. We almost always default to the comfort path of least resistance. Television advertisers for years have used these methods to make us buy products we don't want or need. They take the time to find out what we WANT to hear, what we WANT to be told. They discover if you like our comfort path and they sell to that path. This comfort path is the main reason why 90% of traders lose money.

Just pause for a moment and ask yourself the following question, then consider your inner responses that you pick up on. Do you think there is a mechanical /computerized/guru system that will continually give you profits? If you do, then ask yourself the following question: What would it mean to you to have this?

-Less stress trading?
-Better health?
-Zero emotions when trading?
-More free time?
-Self-esteem?
-Power?
-Material goods?

Just play with this for a moment but REALLY focus internally on how the system would be good for you.

After you have done this you will have come a long way to discovering part of your comfort path. THIS is the path that you will evaluate any trading product on. THIS is how you will be sold the latest trading idea to come down the pipe.

The 10% guy on the other hand does not have a comfort path for trading; he has something far more reliable. Before we get to that, let's consider the points above and how these will affect your trading?
Let's take 'less stress trading' and see how you could satisfy this. How about:

-The latest trading book?
-The latest software idea?
-A tell me what to do subscription?
-A guru's advice?
-A trading course to learn new skills?
-A gossip forum to pick up tips?

Now look back at the list and notice that **any one of them** will 'help' with the earlier blue text areas.

So...the losing 90% are the traders who ultimately believe in the idea that there is an EXTERNAL product/system/concept that will satisfy what they listed under the bulleted points above. The 10% have no such notion of the above, in fact they will make money regardless of any product / system / concept they use.

The 10% have one thing that every single one of the 90% is looking for. The 90% are not looking at the wrong product, the wrong system or the wrong concept. They are simply looking in the wrong place.

IT'S ALL ABOUT WHAT YOU <u>BELIEVE</u> TO BE TRUE RATHER THAT WHAT <u>IS</u> TRUE.

What is a belief? What do you believe to be true?

It might seem at first like this is an easy questions to answer and on the face of it, suppose it is, however once you start to question beliefs, things become not quite so easy to explain. We can say at a simple level that "a belief is something you believe in".

But how do measure a belief? Are there different qualities of beliefs? What will these different beliefs mean to you?

To gain a better understanding you might try a simple exercise.

1. Think of a belief that you hold that we can validate as being 100% true. You MUST start with a belief something like this: The center of the sun is hot.

2. Now is the time to think deeply about this belief, best that you close your eyes and focus on this belief. As you focus on this belief become extremely sensitive to how the belief FEELS to you. You need to do this with the utmost commitment to REALLY monitoring how this belief is represented to the WHOLE of your very being. (You should spend about 3-5 minutes on this first part)

When finished take a pad and write down every physical feeling or sensory perception that you experienced.

3. Next think of another belief (As this is all about trading we will use the belief that you are a successful trader) Again... I cannot stress enough at this point that you need to do this with the utmost commitment to REALLY monitoring how this belief is represented to the WHOLE of your very being. (You should spend about 3-5 minutes on this second part) When finished take a pad and write down every physical feeling or sensory perception that you experienced to do with this belief.

4. When you have completed steps 1-3 take both beliefs and compare them against EVERYTHING that you felt and experienced. If BOTH beliefs compare the same, i.e. your belief that you are a successful trader produced the same experiences that you felt with the belief that the center of the sun is hot then you are already one of the 10% who make vast sums from trading.

If you detect differences then you are almost certainly to be one of the 90%.

I can tell you without doubt that the 10% believe in their ability to make money to the same degree that they believe the sun will rise in the morning.

I can further tell you that this is the ONLY difference between the successful and the unsuccessful.

Every successful trader I have ever met has an intrinsic belief / knowing that he/she IS successful. On the other hand every trader I have ever met who is still searching for successful trading is still looking at:

-The latest all singing all dancing software
-The latest and greatest data feed
-The latest chart pattern
-The very best time frame
-The latest chart indicator (Some software has 1,000's of built in indicators that all work right!
-The latest moving average setting
-The latest guru's offerings
-The latest 'tipster' offering
-Is daily browsing huge trading forums looking for the 'blind' to lead them to wealth?
-This list goes on and forever circles within the 90%

--End--

Thank you, Rakesh, for these words of wisdom. During my trading and investing career I have come to realize you are not only accurate, but also extremely wise. Belief, when we talk about VSA, means believing in yourself and your system. Now I have to admit, at the very beginning as I was learning VSA, I found many of the concepts difficult to grasp.

You must believe in these principles. Don't get me wrong, it's not easy in the beginning. It will be difficult at first, to accept and understand these principles, but the Volume Spread Analysis methodology really does 'demystify the markets' (to quote Tim Rayment, a two-time winner of the World Cup Trading Championship). I often hear customers that have read either one of Tom's books tell me how they finally found a system that lifts the fog on the mechanics of the market.

Fortunately these days, in the VSA Club (www.vsaclub.com), there is a weekly webinar called *"The Closing Bell"*, where fund manager Philip Friston and I find charts that show strong VSA principles with either strength or weakness. Most of our webinars are archived. Club members have access to see the VSA principles on video and additional educational webinars.

If you are new to the VSA club, I can suggest you watch one video in particular. In late April, I did a scan of the metals markets. For some months I felt warning that there was a massive sell-off in the silver market.

The Scanner

VSA CHART 47 shows the results of the weekly scan of the metals markets. The scan shows several signs of weakness as silver approached $50.00. Incidentally, these prices were at the same level as the prices were in January of 1980 during the collapse of silver when the Hunt brothers had cornered the silver market. The results were uncannily accurate.

The indicator scan that I did using TradeGuider EOD at the end of April 2011 showed some extremely unusual activity in the silver markets that caught my attention. As you can see in **VSA CHART 47**, this is seen in any market and you should be on alert to an opportunity to make money.

VSA CHART 47

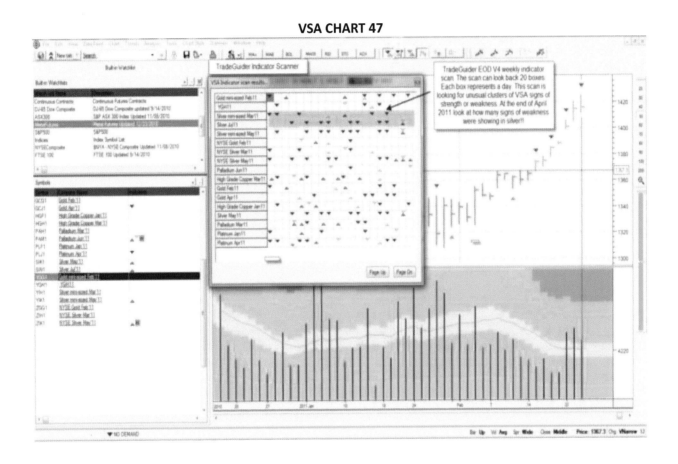

Looking at the chart, note that one of the two strongest *Signs of Weakness* appear a week before the collapse and on **VSA CHART 48**, note the Spread of the bars prior to the *Climactic Action* bar shown at bar A.

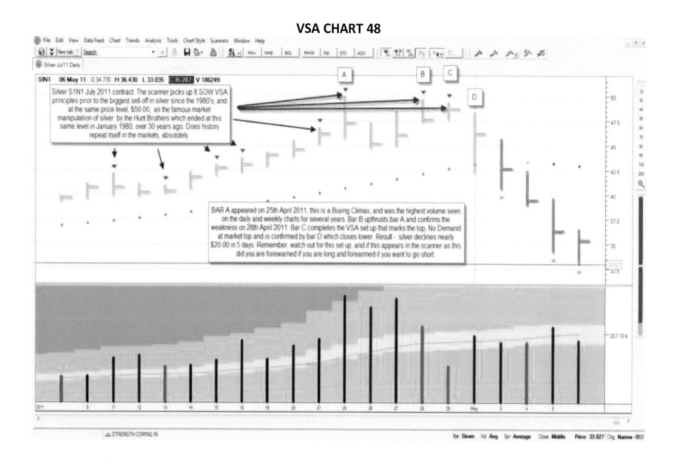

VSA CHART 48

If we take the silver market in May 2011 as an example, the news and reports about silver were extremely bullish. I actually received emails from a number of places encouraging me to get into the bullion market in April 2011. This is exactly the same situation we saw in the oil markets in 2008. If you see a *Buying Climax*, especially when it is confirmed by an *Up-thrust* followed by *No Demand*, this is a set-up that will eventually appear in all markets and time frames. So learn and remember the VSA principles. Once you believe in them, they will not let you down.

We are what we believe. Our thoughts and actions govern our outcomes in life, and yes, this applies to being a trader or investor. We must have faith that we are successful traders and investors who make money, we must accept and have an understanding of 'the game' we are playing, we must apply the five 'P's described earlier in the book, and all of that really can put the odds in your favor in order to make well informed, intelligent, higher probability trading and investing decisions. ***You really can use the Universal Laws to improve your life, your happiness, and your trading and investment performance, but first, you must believe.***

CHAPTER 10
Reasons Why Retail Traders and Investors Lose Money

One of my most successful seminars was entitled, *"10 Ways Volume Spread Analysis Will Turn Losing Traders into Winning Traders"*, which explained how the Smart Money trading patterns can alert you on what is really happening in the markets. In this webinar, I also listed the 10 reasons why I think the average retail trader and investor loses money in the markets:

1. Losing traders do not have a trading plan and trading journal.

As I have stated earlier, it is vital to have a plan and journal of your processes as you trade or invest. Without it, you have no record of what you are doing, whether if it is right or wrong. You want to take note of when you make successful trades in order to recognize certain patterns in your winning strategies. The same goes for losing trades. If you do not keep track of losing trades, how can you learn from your mistakes? Fail to plan, plan to fail!

2. Losing traders do different things on different days and are totally inconsistent.

What causes inconsistency? This branches off from reason number 1- it's either lack of a trading plan, but also, it can be *doubt* in your trading plan. Again, if you don't have a plan, you will most likely try all different types of strategies, in hopes of finding that one magic method. Now if you don't *believe* your trading plan is helpful in making successful trades or investments, you obviously will not follow that plan and use all sorts of other strategies. You may as well not have a plan at all!

3. Losing traders have no belief in their chosen strategy.

As mentioned in reason number 2, belief in what you do is vital to your financial reward. If you believe in your trading plan and are confident in your ability to read the charts, you will always follow your strategy. Do not let fear and doubt steer you from your trading plan. As I have said numerous times, this can happen when the news is bad and everyone starts to panic and sell. Your brain will process this information and ignite emotions of fear and doubt. Most often, your gut instinct will want to follow suit with everyone else, but if you have a plan, know the VSA principles and can read the charts, you will know the truth as to what is really going on in the markets.

4. Losing traders think and act like gamblers.

The majority of traders and investors don't know what truly drives the markets. They take a chance when making their buying or selling decisions if they are unaware of 'the game' and the big institutional money players that are involved. This scenario is much like a Las Vegas casino. The 'House' usually wins, but if a well-trained card counter goes to Vegas, they have the odds in their favor, which is the reason why card counters are banned if discovered. As a trader or investor, you can be the card counter and put the odds in your favor against the 'House', or the Smart Money! All you need to do is study the VSA principles, become confident in your trading plan, and

5. Losing traders are always searching for the Holy Grail of trading and get engrossed with many of the trading products out there that claim to have a high percentage of accuracy.

The uninformed Herd get suckered into this 'Holy Grail' idea because they either want to make lots of money and/or they are tired of losing money. We have all heard the claims. There are companies out there that tell us exactly what we want to hear as a traders and investor. Many promise that their system guarantees accuracy of 80% or more and confuse losing traders that end up trying several of these different systems, which almost always result in losses. If there were such a thing, wouldn't everyone use it? How many times have you been burned?

6. Losing traders often use too many systems and an overabundance of indicators, so they never know what the chart is really telling them.

Have you ever suffered from 'analysis paralysis'? Again, the chart never lies if you know how to read it correctly. If there are several different indicators and a variety of charts, it is natural for your brain to experience information overload, which will confuse you causing your mental clarity to disappear. Make trading and investing as simple as possible by using the tried and tested methods, such as VSA and the Wyckoff method that help you read the market as it unfolds.

7. Losing traders are often under-capitalized and take large trades with poor risk/reward ratios with no money management skills. They also have difficulty accepting losses.

Winning traders believe in themselves, lack fear, and have discipline, as well as the knowledge of how the markets work. They are realistic and plan accordingly. They know they can never be 100% right and get out of losing positions quickly, already prepared to take a possible small business loss and prevent a large financial disaster. How do you treat your losses?

8. Losing traders do not understand how markets work and they often believe that price moves markets.

Winning traders have studied for years on how the markets truly operate. It is the forces of supply and demand, along with the trading of the Smart Money that cause prices to move. The professionals have years of experience and know how to play the 'game' in order to win.

9. Losing traders always follow everyone else becoming one with the uninformed Herd and get locked in to bad trades.

To become a winning trader, you must prevent yourself from becoming a member of the Herd. Do not get slaughtered by the Smart Money! Once you truly comprehend how the 'game' is played and understand how to correctly read a price chart, it won't be long for you to become a winner in trading the markets.

10. It is all about discipline.

Fortunately, you don't have to be a genius to be a successful trader and investor. In 1999, Warren Buffett, Berkshire Hathaway Chief and investor extraordinaire, was interviewed by *Business Week*. He said, "Success in investing doesn't correlate with IQ once you're above the level of 25. Once you have ordinary intelligence, what you need is the temperament to control the urges that get the other people into trouble when investing." It's true that everyone cannot be gifted with Buffett's calm, cool demeanor, but he is spot-on when he says it is necessary to avoid your own worst instincts because that will be what helps you reach your financial goals, temperament and control.

Winning traders have a pattern and share many common traits. I have noticed that most have several of the following characteristics:

- Winners believe in themselves.

- Winners have the power of visualization and the ability to see the winners and cut the losers.

- Winners are contrarian. They do not follow the Herd and they think as an individual.

- Winners have expert chart reading skills. They are extremely experienced and have developed their skills throughout their trading and investing careers.

- Winners are intensely disciplined and have temperament and control.

- Winners are spiritual in their own individual way.

- Winners are open-minded and are willing to help others.

- Winners expect to receive and they do so, graciously.

- Winners have excellent risk management strategies.

- Winners are always able to stay in the game.

- Winners take consistent and small profits. They are never greedy.

- Winners are always positive, happy, and content.

There is a great story recounted by futures broker, Martin Wong in Malaysia, by which he compares the similarities between trading and investing in the markets.

The story is *"Ali Baba and the Forty Thieves"*, which is tale about a man named Ali Baba and his older brother Cassim. They are the sons of a merchant. As the story goes, their father dies. Soon after, Cassim greedily marries a rich woman and becomes wealthier as he builds onto their father's business. Ali Baba, on the other hand, marries a poor woman and settles into the trade of a woodcutter.

One day, Ali Baba goes to work collecting and cutting firewood in the forest. While on his mission, Ali Baba happens to overhear a group of forty thieves visiting their hidden treasure trove. The treasure is in an enchanted cave that can open or close by using certain magical phrases. It opens on the words, "iftah ya simsim", which in English, is commonly known as "open sesame". To bar the entrance, it seals on the words "close, simsim", or "close sesame". When the thieves leave, Ali Baba enters the cave alone and takes some of the treasure home.

In order to weigh this new wealth of gold coins, Ali Baba borrows his sister-in-law's scale. Unbeknownst to Ali, she puts a blob of wax in the scale to find out what he is using them for because he is curious to know what kind of grain her impoverished brother-in-law needs to measure. To her shock, she finds a gold coin sticking to the scale and tells her greedy husband. Cassim, with his horribly selfish nature, forces Ali Baba to reveal the location and the secret of the cave. Cassim goes to the treasure trove and enters with the magic words, but in his ravenous excitement over the treasures, he forgets the magic words to exit the cave. He gets stuck and the thieves find him there and kill him.

It is easy to go into the market. You don't need magic words, but all you do you need is a computer with an internet connection, a brokerage account, and some charting tools. Knowing when to get out is what is most important. Greed and excitement, as highlighted in the story of Ali Baba, will cost you money. In the unfortunate case of Cassim, it cost him his life in this famous story. Become the master of your emotions each time you trade and invest. Follow your plan with military precision and discipline, knowing exactly what to do if anything does not go according to your trading plan.

SUMMARY
List of Key Points I Want You to Remember from the Previous Chapters

- We are each unique in our own way. We all may have different account sizes, loss tolerance levels, experience levels, different perspectives, and different levels of self-discipline.

- The VSA strategies are a guide, but must be adapted to your style of trading and personality. Only you can do that for yourself.

- VSA principles apply to all markets where there is Volume available and in all time frames including futures, commodities, stocks, spot forex, etc.

- KISS stands for Keep It Simple, Stupid! This is not rocket science. VSA is very logical and is based on principles that have been around for over a century.

- Take a holistic approach to your chart analysis. By this, I mean you should emphasize the importance of the entire whole, as well as the interdependence of its individual parts.

- Strength can appear on down bars.

- Weakness can appear on up bars.

- The background analysis of the chart is vital.

- Has the strength or weakness appeared at the top or bottom of a channel?

- Is this a major trend reversal or a retracement?

- Is the news good or bad?

- Is demand overcoming supply?

- Is supply overcoming demand?

- All patterns seen in the past eventually will be at the right edge of your chart, but they will come in different intensities.

- VSA is a discretionary methodology that still requires discipline and money management.

- VSA is much more effective when used with support and resistance, or the Wyckoff method.

- You must use more than one time frame to see the bigger picture.

- If you listen to the news, you must have a very contrarian view of the contents when taking a position.

- The chart never lies. Develop and improve your charting reading skills.

- Become familiar with the 'personality' of the instruments you trade.

- Always use a stop loss. You can never be 100% right.

- Always pay extra attention to ultra high or ultra low Volume on the chart when it appears.

- Look for the Smart Money activity. Ask yourself why they are active or inactive.

- Many VSA patterns require 2 or 3 bars for confirmation. Do not rush in your decisions.

- Volume is the key to the truth.

- Learn how to trade with Point & Figure in order to see graphically the uncontaminated areas of supply and demand. Correlate and cross-reference P&F with VSA for even higher probability trades.

CHAPTER 11
Interviews with International Wyckoff and Volume Spread Analysis Experts

Interview 1: David Weis

 **David Weis (D) is a world-renowned Wyckoff expert and contributor to www.richardwyckoff.org where he runs a course on Point & Figure charting. His book, *"Trades About to Happen: A Modern Adaptation of the Wyckoff Method"* is due to be published in 2012.**

GH: How did you get involved in trading and investing in the markets?

DW: I was working in Louisiana whilst studying for a PhD in English Literature. One day I saw graffiti that gave me a sobering lesson in the law of supply and demand: English teachers are a dime a dozen! Although I had planned to stay in academic life, a visit to a friend in the research department of a commodity brokerage company in our hometown of Memphis, Tennessee, made me change my mind. I joined the technical research department, compiling charts by hand, and was soon making money; by the time the markets heated up in 1970 I had become a technical analyst, and carried on from there.

GH: That sounds very much like Tom Williams. He began as a chartist for a hedge fund in Beverly Hills. And how long have you been trading and investing?

DW: For 40 years, since 1971.

GH: Now you're an acknowledged expert in Wyckoff methodology, and Point and Figure charting. How did you come across the work of Wyckoff, and why is his work still so valuable to traders today?

DW: In those days, people who knew about and profited from Wyckoff had a tendency to keep it to themselves. I learned about it from one of my accountants and they very kindly arranged and paid for my tuition. It did not take long for my new knowledge to pay me substantial dividends!

GH: Again, much like Tom Williams, he also studied Wyckoff. Now, the thing about the Wyckoff method is that it's not a 'Black Box' approach. Can you describe, or summarize, the Wyckoff method of trading?

DW: In the Wyckoff method you're listening to what the market says about itself and acting on market-generated information. There's no interaction with any mathematical information, the news, or any tips about the future, but just solely what the market says about itself. The essence of the method is to develop an intuitive judgment based on close and prolonged study of market movements. Although Wyckoff lived in the days of ticker tape when trading was confined mainly to stocks and commodities, his method is just as applicable to chart reading and the much greater range of tradable instruments that we have today.

GH: Why do you think the Wyckoff method becoming so popular again?

DW: I think there is now a greater understanding of the limitations of mathematically generated indicators. Such indicators try to predict the future by analyzing the past, but experience shows that they are far from infallible. The main problem with indicators such as MACD, Stochastics, and RSI, is that they are lagging indicators. Traders are now realizing that the key to success lies in learning what the market is telling you at the leading edge of the chart, in order to predict with a high degree of certainty which way the market will move in the future.

GH: So, what are some of the things Wyckoff would encourage us to look at when analyzing the market?

DW: Essentially, Wyckoff was interested in the Spread of the price bar, the position of the close, and the Volume. Also of interest were the duration of moves and the interaction of the price bars with trend lines, support and resistance lines, and channels.

GH: This is much the same as what VSA is about: the Spread of the bar, the Volume, the Closing Price in relation to that Volume, and analysis of the background. Thus, we get to certain support and resistance levels (what I call trigger numbers) where those levels form an area of high probability trading, because everything is lining up in your favor.

My next question is on Point & Figure charting, which many readers may not be familiar with. Can you tell us a bit about it and why it can be relevant in today's markets?

DW: Point & Figure seems to have fallen out of favor today, but Wyckoff, in his first course, says that this is the most important chart to maintain. If you study the course you will see just how much emphasis there is on Point & Figure.

A bar chart shows the price spread and the open and close for the period in question; be it days, weeks or whatever. The Point & Figure chart on the other hand, easily enables you to adjust your analysis by changing the box sizes and the reversal factor.

Point & Figure charting is superb in its ability to reduce market noise. For example, select a box size of 10 pips x 3 boxes. This means that we plot three boxes only when the market has moved (10x3) = 30 pips in either direction (up or down). This methodology eliminates market noise and enables the trader to get a better view of market dynamics. As a little bit of background on a very large subject, Point & Figure was plotted early in its history as depicting market price movement with a series of X's and O's. These days it is more popularly shown as different colored boxes.

For those interested in the development history of Point & Figure, Richard Wyckoff's book, *"Stock Market Techniques"* published in 1933 stated that the 'one point figure chart' is the standard for stocks.

To Wyckoff, the most important thing about the Point & Figure chart were the horizontal areas, or the lines of congestion, from which you can make a Point & Figure target projection of the extent of a move. Point & Figure charts give very reliable buy and sell signals, and perhaps more importantly, it can indicate the breakout direction of the market above or below the congestion areas, in effect, showing the trader exactly where the cause was being built for an effect.

You'd combine the use of a standard bar chart and Volume to get additional confirmation of the future direction. Point & Figure charts also give reliable price targets, as well as show the VSA corroborative situation by virtue of the fact that a line of up-boxes clearly shows demand and a line of down-boxes indicates supply.

In summary, Point & Figure is measuring the cause and potential and the strength of the lateral movement from which to project up or down.

GH: So, as far as it is going to help the trader, the Point & Figure chart is going to help him select a Point & Figure signal which will form the basis of where to eventually take profit, a point which may, indeed, be much further away than one chosen without the aid of Point & Figure.

We could conclude by saying that Point & Figure accurately depicts the precise price levels where price has reversed or gone up, which in effect can therefore be regarded as graphically showing price activity Volume. It is this Volume that can be correlated to the various trading signals that are given out by TradeGuider, based on the software's analysis of the Volume at the chosen price level. The proper and combined use of Point & Figure with TradeGuider will lessen the amount of Volume analysis needed to take high probability trades, and by implication, will reduce even further the chances of making analytical mistakes or misinterpretations.

Interview 2: Philip Friston

 **Philip Friston (PF) is a professional hedge fund manager, as well as a Volume Spread Analysis expert and educator.**

GH: How did you first become involved in the financial markets and what led you to Volume Spread Analysis?

PF: I became interested in the late 1960s. My father ran an investment company and I also had a friend that was interested in shares. I was too young to have shares directly, so my father would buy shares and I would own a portion of these. I didn't really know anything about the markets at that time - I just thought that it was better than putting money in the bank. It was around 1974 when the market lost around 78% of its value in 18 months. It was then that I lost half of my savings and came to realize that I had to learn what was going on. I applied myself to the study of the markets and got involved with technical analysis. After trying out various bits of software with only limited success, I was persuaded to try a program called *Genie Chartist*, which was the forerunner to TradeGuider.

I liked what I saw. The program seemed straightforward in the sense that there was just a bar chart with Volume activity displayed underneath. There were no indicators such as moving averages or Stochastics. It was based upon supply and demand, which I understood from economics. I thought this could be the answer. As a result of attending Tom Williams' seminars I finally realized what was going on in the markets and decided to concentrate entirely on VSA.

GH: What do you think is the difference, if there is one, between standard technical analysis that obviously looks at the price, and VSA?

PF: VSA tells you what is happening in real time and if you analyze the background you should gain a picture of the general trend of the market. I know of no other system or method of technical analysis that will do that reliably.

GH: Until you found Tom Williams, did you have any other mentors?

PF: No. In a business where it is notoriously difficult to find a really reliable system - the Holy Grail, if you will - I would say Tom was the first and only person whom I actually trusted. You have to accept that as an investor or trader you are going to make losses. Even the professionals do.

GH: How do you explain your success with VSA for over 20 years?

PF: I think it was when I ceased looking at bars in just one dimension. If I saw a down bar with very, very high Volume I thought that it must mean that buying was coming in, especially if the bar closed off its low, but the most important point I was missing was that there would also be lots of selling on the same bar. I was only looked at the bar in one dimension, not two. In fact, you shouldn't be buying on a bar like that because often, there is too much selling present for prices to go up. The selling could swamp the buying and take prices lower still.

GH: So, a down bar such as you have described does not give a signal to buy instantly?

PF: No. You've got to be patient. And equally, if you reverse it and turn it upside down, you wouldn't go short on a very high Volume up bar. In both cases you would wait for confirmation.

GH: Tom says that he doesn't look too much at fundamentals because the chart reveals what the professionals are thinking. I know that you look at what the market's doing and you look at news. Could you tell us how you use fundamental analysis in conjunction with VSA to confirm that the market is doing what you expect?

PF: I use fundamentals to weed out stocks that don't meet my criteria. For example, I would not consider a company with a high level of debt, but is the chart that will tell me whether a stock is good or bad. By using a top down approach, I try to reduce my risk to an acceptable level. To place too much weight on fundamentals could be misleading. A stock might appear bad because the market hasn't yet caught up with what the chart is telling you.

GH: Do you use any form of technical analysis to confirm VSA, or the other way round, and if you do, what do you use?

PF: Not really. The only one that I do use, the RSI, which is a momentum indicator, can be quite useful to confirm VSA. I only use it in limited circumstances, which I won't go into here, because I think that any such tool, if used all the time, won't work.

GH: What would be your favorite VSA signal, for example, to go long?

PF: My favorite is to see a down move in a particular stock. You see accumulation or buying taking place in the background, and then you see the price move back down to that area where you had seen the previous buying. When you see that, we call it a *Test*. This is a down bar, preferably with a narrow Spread, with relatively low Volume compared to the accumulation area to the left. What this is telling us is that as the price falls back down into the area of accumulation, any selling or supply that was present has now dried up.

GH: BP would be a good example of that. Perhaps we can discuss that stock in a little more detail. Prices plummeted for several weeks to an eight-year low. We even heard rumors that BP was going bust and yet it was a great stock to buy. Most people would not believe that statement, but if we look at the chart, it doesn't lie. Describe what's going on here.

PF: According to the fundamentals, the company was quite solid. Bullish, even, but the news put out was so bearish that it created an atmosphere of panic. The Herd or the uninformed investors were terrified of losing their money and were prepared to sell at any price. That is when the Smart Money stepped in and said, "Thank you very much. This looks like a good long-term stock. We've got the opportunity to buy it now at a very cheap price."

GH: Can you tell us more about the relationship between the Herd and the Smart Money?

PF: To give you an example, during a bull market as prices go up, more and more people will be sucked in. What is happening is that the Smart Money is selling to the Herd at ever rising prices in order to keep the bull market going. The Herd keep buying because they believe the good news that is being spread around and do not wish to miss out on a good thing. Eventually, there comes a point when prices get pushed up so high that they are completely overbought. At that point the professionals start selling. Then, later, when the market falls back to oversold levels, they begin to buy in again.

GH: And that's exactly what VSA determines. It sees when the professionals are buying or selling and when the Herd are involved. Is that what causes the very high Volume, the interaction of the Herd and the Smart Money?

PF: It is. At the bottom of the market, it's the fear of losing money that is causing the Herd to sell every stock they've got to get their money back that creates the high Volume. At the top of the market, it's the opposite. It is greed and the fear of missing out on further gains. We know that these gains won't materialize; however new people coming into the market don't know that.

GH: If you see a VSA signal like the one you have just described, namely, a down bar with a wide spread, maybe with bad news and a *Test*, would you enter a trade every time or are there times when you would wait?

PF: This is where experience tells you to learn to recognize certain situations where patience is called for. However, in general, I would probably go in and buy, but not if I were trading, say, a future. After all, with the bank paying no interest on your deposit, it is worth buying a stock with a decent and reasonably secure return. You get paid for owning the stock and you might even earn some money on the investment, as well. I would put my stop loss below the area of accumulation. If the stock then starts going up and we see *Signs of Weakness* coming in, I would probably sell half of the holding.
Then if it comes back down to the bottom again and *Tests*, I would buy that half back again. And then eventually, if the market goes up, I'm fully in.

The advantage of doing that is if it goes up and down a couple of times like that, and then drops below the stop loss because perhaps the accumulation hasn't worked, which can happen sometimes, hopefully the amount I have made on the gains would cover any losses I've made . So overall I wouldn't lose anything.

GH: Many traders and investors don't really understand what risk means. How do you understand the work 'risk' and what risk parameters do you use when you take a position?

PF: Risk is one of the most important factors in the market. You can pick good stocks and still lose money if you don't get the risk right. It's a question of looking at risk and reward in every purchase you make. You've got to get that right. I work on a certain level of risk that I'm prepared to accept. If I see a stock on which the risk is too high, I don't buy it.

GH: Let us say that your capital account was $100,000. How much would you be prepared to risk in any one position?

PF: From an investment point of view, I would probably want to invest in perhaps 40 stocks, which is 2.5% of your capital base per position. I feel this is a nice manageable position. Once you go too far above that, say if you are managing 80-100 stocks, it becomes a little bit too cumbersome.

GH: Tom mentioned 3%. I prefer 2.5%, like you. So you don't want to be exposing yourself to saying, as many traders do, that "Here is a golden opportunity, I got three tips that this is going up, my account is one hundred thousand. I'll tell you what, it's such a good tip, and I'll put $50,000 in here." That's not good advice.

PF: That's too much risk going into one stock. If you are wrong, then you are going to lose too much capital and it will affect your confidence.

GH: What is the worst loss that you can remember? Even if you can't remember exactly what the figure was, do you remember how you felt after that loss, and how do you deal with emotion when you invest?

PF: I do remember the loss, but not the amount or even the stock. It was in 1987 when the market dropped dramatically over two or three days. With hindsight, I can see why I shouldn't have been in certain stocks.

GH: The second half of my question is as a fund manager, how do you control your own emotions when you manage not only your own, but other people's money? Losses can make us depressed, angry and resentful, to name but a few emotions. You always seem to be very calm, collected and disciplined.

PF: It's no longer a problem with investing because I have been doing it for so long. A loss doesn't worry me, it's just par for the course. I'm not afraid to admit that I do have losses, quite frequently in fact, but that's all part of it. I've learned now, because I've been doing this for so long, that if I make a loss, I will make a profit later on. Perhaps I should emphasize that I am speaking from my experience and confidence as an investor. With trading, it might be another matter!

GH: So you define trading and investing as two different things. In Tom's day, there was mainly the stock market and commodities; it was end-of-day with the ticker tape and no computers. He was telling a story of Teledyne where he was short and the ticker tape was going up, but it turned out to be an *Up-thrust*. There is a difference now because people can trade a 1 minute chart, be in and out of the market, and make $500 up to $20,000 in minutes. Then, of course, you have the investment that can make the same amount of money but it takes six months. That means there's a big difference between investing and trading. Do you think VSA applies equally to both types of trading?

PF: Certainly. VSA can work equally well on a monthly, a 5 minute, and, if you have enough liquidity, even a 1 minute chart. We've seen it on the E-mini S&P futures. The principles are exactly the same for charts of all timeframes.

GH: What do you think the general public's misconceptions are of the market? We have touched on market manipulation. I was very skeptical of that whole concept when Tom told me about it, but I know better now. How can you give the general public some advice to 'wake up', as Richard Ney put it, to what's going on?

PF: I think the biggest problem with the general public is that they tend to get into things too late. They are reading the financial press, they read all the general news, and thereby don't get into the market at the right time. It's very difficult. It goes against human instinct to buy a stock when the news is bad. Equally, it goes against human instinct to sell a stock when the news is very good. It's the total opposite to the way in which we are programmed or conditioned as human beings. You almost have to re-program yourself in order to follow VSA!

GH: That's almost exactly what Tom once said to me. He said, "If you do everything against your gut instinct when you're trading, you're going to make money!"

So, we've talked about VSA and how it has helped you and investing. Can you now give me three simple rules that you'd give a trader or investor just coming into the market, or three simple trading rules that will keep people out of trouble and, hopefully, make them some money?

PF: Yes I can.

For one, **risk management**. This is extremely important, because, if you haven't any risk management you're very likely, if not certain, to lose money however good you are at picking stocks.

Second, **discipline**. You have to be disciplined to do your analysis thoroughly, to follow it, and not be influenced by other things around you, particularly the news.

Number 3, **Follow Volume Spread Analysis**!

GH: And read the chart!

PF: Yes, read the chart. That makes four.

GH: Do you think chart reading is a language, like French or English or Spanish?

PF: I think it is. You can learn so much on your own, but to be really fluent, you need to go and live in the country concerned, in other words, to immerse yourself in VSA. There are many things you can do, including joining the VSA Club. You can get a hold of lots of charts. Go back several hundred bars, say 500, which you can do on TradeGuider, then pick a point way back and analyze the chart up to the right edge. Move along a day at a time to see if you are correct. Re-analyze as you go. Don't look ahead first though. Every time you get it wrong, ask yourself why.

You must practice. If you have question, and there is no such thing as a dumb question when it comes to VSA, you can post it in the VSA Club forum where most questions are answered within 24 hours.

GH: If everybody in the world who was a trader or investor had VSA and the TradeGuider software, would the market change or stay the same?

PF: It would change if they all understood it, but I think in reality that is never going to happen.

GH: I once asked Tom the same question and he said, "There are so many different markets, so many different timeframes, and so many different people that even if it did happen, it would be applied at different times, and of course, it wouldn't have an effect on the market because the market is moved by supply and demand.

Finally, just to wrap up, with your lifetime trading experience, what advice would you give to someone who has just started out, or has been losing money using technical and fundamentals tools, and just can't figure it out and simply wants to lift the fog off the market? What's that path moving forward?

PF: First of all they should join the VSA Club and learn from it. There's a lot of material in there including a lot of webinars they can look at. Yes there is a monthly subscription, but you can't learn about the markets for free! After all, it's a lot cheaper to join the VSA Club than it is to go into the markets blind and try to trade by yourself. You'll lose lots of money - thousands, or, in a few cases, millions.

If you wanted to set up a shop somewhere, you wouldn't just go and purchase the first shop you saw in the estate agent's window. You would want to do your homework. You would want to find out about the area and the particular business you're going into. You'd want to ask yourself if there any competitors or will there likely be, in the near future and if so, can I find a way of bettering those competitors and gain their custom?

But on the other hand, with trading, we tend to think we can open an account, start trading without any knowledge, and expect to make money. It simply cannot happen. You need to treat it as a business, do your homework, and study it carefully in order to make money.

GH: What you really need is a business plan as a trader. In fact, fail to plan, plan to fail!

Interview 3: Dr. Gary Dayton

 **Dr. Gary Dayton (GD) is a professional trader and Wyckoff expert, as well as a licensed psychologist.**

GH: How did you first get involved with trading and investing?

GD: Back in the late 90's I ordered a brochure from Ken Roberts, which really intrigued me. I stayed up all night reading it two or three times over. I just couldn't believe what he was describing. Of course, it took a lot more than just that kind of material for me to be good at it, but that was how I started.

GH: You are now recognized around the world as a Wyckoff expert and you have done several seminars on Volume Spread Analysis techniques. How did you come across the teachings of Wyckoff and also those of Tom Williams? How do you account for the renewed interest in the Wyckoff method over the past two or three years?

GD: My trading wasn't successful at first. One day, when I was in a trading chat room run by Linda Raschke, she said, "If you really want to understand technical analysis, you need to read Wyckoff. Wyckoff covers about 90% of technical analysis." She had taken the Wyckoff course herself and uses a lot of Wyckoff methodology. That intrigued me. I've always been the kind of person who needs to know the reasons.

So began my quest to learn about Wyckoff. In the 90's, there wasn't much information available on line, so I ordered the course from the Wyckoff Stock Market Institute and studied it. During my studies I came across Tom Williams' book, *"The Undeclared Secrets that Drive the Stock Market"*. The £50 I spent on a copy was just about the best money that I ever spent on my trading education. I read and re-read that book many times and have actually rewritten it, including the charts, in my own words - not to take authorship, but just to have a better understanding of it.

Wyckoff's original course and Tom Williams' book are the foundation of my studies. I then met David Weis and I became his student. From David, a world-renowned Wyckoff expert, I learned of the awe in which the method was held when he was first mastering it.

As for your second question, yes, it really is significant, and I think 'awesome' is a fair description. It tells us how the market works, based on the laws of supply and demand, and how it can be influenced by the actions of the larger players. Now, thanks to Wyckoff and Williams, Weis and a few others, we have a chance to interpret the tracks left by the big players and to follow in their steps.

GH: Wyckoff uses the term 'Composite Operator' in his books. Could you explain what he meant by this?

GD: Wyckoff is conveying the idea that a good way to understand the market is to regard it as a single entity (even though we know, of course, that it is made up of multiple individuals). This hypothetical operator is managing the market in terms of supply and demand, building up a line of stock through accumulation, or selling it for distribution. If, for example, there has been panic selling as the market falls, perhaps for days, or even weeks on end, and then suddenly, we see a large amount of activity and the market closes down on massively increased Volume, this is a clue that the Composite Operator of the market has decided, 'Prices have fallen far enough, it is now time to support this market.' BP is an excellent case in point.

GH: Do you think the Wyckoff method, formulated around 100 years ago for stock trading, is only suitable for stock traders or does it work in every market?

GD: It works in all markets, including futures, commodities and forex, in all timeframes. This is because Wyckoff shows us that the principles of market behavior are based on human behavior. He was really talking about human behavior in the context of freely traded markets. It doesn't matter what the market is trading as reflected in the charts of those markets. As a psychologist, I know human behavior doesn't change materially over the centuries or even millennia. Changes in human behavior are evolutionary, not revolutionary. Changes in information technology may be revolutionary, but the ways we respond to them are evolutionary. That is why Wyckoff remains fresh and relevant today.

GH: How do you think VSA has enhanced Wyckoff's original work?

GD: I think Tom did a brilliant job, particularly in simplifying Wyckoff's sometimes-complex work. Mastering Wyckoff takes time and dedication, which is a bit like learning to play chess to a high standard! Also, Tom makes it clear that the market, as described by Wyckoff, isn't just a transfer of stock from strong players to weak players, but it is also a transfer of risk. The strong players understand that when the market rallies to a certain level, it becomes too risky to hold on to their stock any longer, so they unload it. These professionals, the Smart Money, look to unload in an active market. When the public, the Herd, get involved and are attracted by the high prices, their involvement is being reflected in the increased Volume on the charts.

GH: How do you think Wyckoff would have interpreted the silver market in May 2011?

GD: I don't know quite how dramatic he would have considered that move to be, but he certainly would have seen the potential for silver to move down after the public had been attracted into the market by the ever-rising prices. It was a perfect opportunity for the Composite Operator to unload all the silver that they had bought further down. You will recall that they unloaded their stock at $50 per once the same price that it had been in the 1980's.

Since 1973, the price had been forced up from $1.95 an ounce to a high of $54 by the Hunt brothers. They had accumulated half of the world's deliverable supply. Then the price plummeted to below $11, bankrupting the Hunts. This raises the question of why silver should have hit $50 and then plummeted on two occasions, despite inflation during the intervening 30 years. My explanation, as a psychologist, is that $50 is a psychologically significant level. Round numbers are often significant; consciously or unconsciously people 'anchor' to them and respond to them in their market behavior.

GH: I refer to those round numbers as *Trigger Numbers* in my book because that's exactly what they are. If you see a price level going back to the same price area and then you see an unusual swell of Volume coming in as we saw in the TradeGuider charts, what you are seeing is a *Buying Climax*, followed two days later by *No Demand*. This is quite interesting and always confuses many traders. Can you explain why weakness appears with very high or ultra high Volume up bars, and then appears again a few bars later with low Volume up bars?

GD: It is confusing and it can seem daunting for novice traders. Even though it sounds contradictory, my recommendation is to persevere because eventually they will understand. Professional traders need an active broad market to unload their stock, whatever it may be, and so the *Buying Climax* occurs when we have weaker holders rush into the market, tempted by rising prices and favorable news. The Smart Money sees the increasing Volume caused by the entry of the Herd into the market and sell into this active buying. We can identify the climax by the way in which the high up bar closes. It will usually close somewhere off the high, closer to the middle, or even down on the lows. The Spread will be wide, indicating heavy activity. Most telling is that we're going to see a very, very large Volume, or ultra high Volume, as VSA would indicate. That is how we know that the Smart Money is unloading into an active market.

Remember however, that an up bar on high Volume is not in itself a signal to sell. We need to see the complete package, which is high Volume bars with a wide Spread, closing mid-range or lower after a move has been underway for some time. At the beginning of a move, high Volume is generally considered to be a positive sign, but negative at the end. Bear in mind that market reversals are not abrupt events. They are more of a process, part of which is a testing to make sure there is no further demand. Finally, once the market has reacted to the *Buying Climax*, it will rally. Wyckoff described this - a *Buying Climax*, a reaction, and a rally - as a topping process, in order to confirm that there really was weakness coming into the market and that the climax was, in fact, a *Buying Climax* and that buying is exhausted. We want to see light Volume and *No Demand*, characterized by lack of Volume and narrower spreads. At that point, we can look for an opportunity to short the market.

GH: That's a perfect explanation. I have two more questions. First, how important is it for traders to have belief in their system to enable them to trade the markets successfully?

GD: I would say it's vitally important. If you don't have confidence in your method and if you don't have confidence in yourself as a trader, you will find trading very difficult. For example, if the market isn't cooperating with your trade entry, you must have the confidence that you can manage your way out of the trade without having a huge loss. If you don't have belief in your method, whether it is Wyckoff/VSA or any other method, you're going to be lost as a trader.

That is because you are always going to be looking to fine-tune and improve your system. You'll likely always be checking the MACD, the RSI, or looking to some other indicator for your confidence. You'll do that because you really don't have confidence in your own abilities.

Also, when you do that, you'll start getting conflicting information. The MACD won't give you the same information as VSA, for example. Now you are left even more confused. It's like having more than one clock. Which clock is telling the right time? You don't really know, and that's going to cause further doubt. It'll create a vicious circle in your belief system. You are just not going to know, but you keep looking and looking. In that process of constantly looking, you are never going to gain confidence in your trading and your system.

You first need to test what works for you, MACD, VSA, Wyckoff or whatever. Once you have decided what works for you, discard the others. Then get to know your chosen method inside and out and become an expert in it. That is the hallmark of professional traders. They are true experts in their chosen method. As your expertise increases, your belief in your method and belief in yourself as a trader is only going to grow to the point where you really do become a competent trader.

GH: And my last question is what would be the next step for someone who has just discovered the Wyckoff method and VSA?

GD: For sure you would want to read both the Wyckoff course and Tom Williams' book, *"The Undeclared Secrets that Drive the Stock Market"*. You should also look at a book edited by Jack Hutson, *"The Wyckoff Method: Charting the Stock Market"*, where you will find a couple of chapters on trading bonds by David Weis. This is brilliant work. Also avail yourself of the great resources online, like the VSA Club through TradeGuider. That is a terrific resource with excellent information on Wyckoff and the VSA method. My website, is another resource where I often post on the Wyckoff method.

In a few weeks, we will be launching a new website called www.richardwyckoff.org that has new software and educational materials on the Wyckoff method. I would encourage traders interested in Wyckoff to look at that. It's all there for traders to acquire and learn and integrate into their own trading. It's the best method that I've ever come across and I have studied an awful lot of stuff. Traders are lucky today since they have both Wyckoff and VSA, which complement one another so nicely. I don't know what else to say about it. It's just the best there is.

Interview 4: Sebastian Manby

Sebastian is a professional trader and Volume Spread Analysis expert.

GH: When and why did you first get interested in trading and investing?

SB: It was in the 80s, right before the '87 crash. I found a print-out of a stock portfolio on the street. It caught my interest and I studied it very closely. But, being only in my teens, I did not have the capital to trade stocks myself.

GH: How did you find out about Tom Williams and VSA?

SB: I used to buy the *Financial Times* on a Saturday and read it through, mainly looking for direction for the following week. I realized later that either journalists don't know how the market works, or professional traders try to trip them up to mislead the public. Anyway, Tom had an advert in the paper, and I called him and requested the info, which he sent to me. I actually still have it.

GH: What was it about VSA that made you study it in so much detail?

SB: The info that Tom sent me talked about floor traders and insiders. Well, I knew nothing about trading, but I had the common sense to know who was behind it all. Most of all, I wanted to make money. The more money I lost, the more determined I was to succeed. I guess it became an obsession, rather than a hobby.

GH: You wrote an article, *"Making Volume Work for You"*. Why is Volume so important on a price chart?

SB: Volume is the key to both the imbalances in traders' positions and also the psychology behind the market. You become a student of human behavior without realizing it. Volume is also very powerful for detecting professional activity, or the lack of it. For example, once the market had shaken out at a certain level, professional traders would then dump blocks of stock to flush out short sellers. If there was still sufficient demand, prices would not fall, because other professional traders being bullish would step in and buy, telling the originators of the selling that the market was still bullish and that higher prices could be expected. We call this a *Test of Supply*, and this will usually be into the same price level as the shakeout.

GH: Why do you think VSA is not as popular as standard technical analysis tools such as MACD, moving averages, and candles?

SB: There are several reasons. VSA is hard to learn and interpret. Most people give up before getting anywhere with it. It takes commitment, determination and patience to learn; you have to be committed, and have the drive to succeed. It takes many hundreds of hours of study. It is not something you can learn in an hour and then go out make money- well, unless you are super smart! Most traders want someone to tell them what to buy or sell, and when; they don't want to do the work themselves.

Even at the turn of the last century, Wyckoff found this in his brokerage: small lot traders would often buy on tips and rumors, very few could read the ticker tape and most would just pray that they would make a profit. The best traders could read the tape, and would often go into a trance-like state when doing so. They were the ones who made all the money, but they never taught anyone else how to do it. Even now, Wyckoff experts tend to keep to themselves, and since there are not many practitioners, it follows that there are not many educators.

There is also a psychological reason. Most new traders forget everything they learned when in an actual trade. Their stress level increases, especially if they are talking a loss, and they go into survival mode, with gut instinct taking over. In such conditions easily learned candlesticks and mathematical indicators, often with automatic alarms, even if all of these are not fully understood, create a welcome comfort zone well away from the intellectual rigor of VSA.

When learning VSA you need to do it in stages. You start with one principle, then progress to the next, and so on. The best way is to print charts and mark on the principles you see. Eventually, it will all come together and with time you will make progress. That's how I did it, but it took years of study. I wonder how many would be as determined as I was!

GH: How long did it take before Tom acknowledged you as a VSA expert?

SB: It was a gradual progression through years of on and off study. After one break of a few weeks, it just seemed to click. It got very easy after that and I began to see things that I could not see before. It was as if someone had opened the floodgates and just saw how the whole market worked.

GH: What is your favorite VSA trade set-up to the long side?

SB: A secondary reaction at a higher low than the previous low, which must be a *Shakeout* or *Selling Climax*.

Chart 1

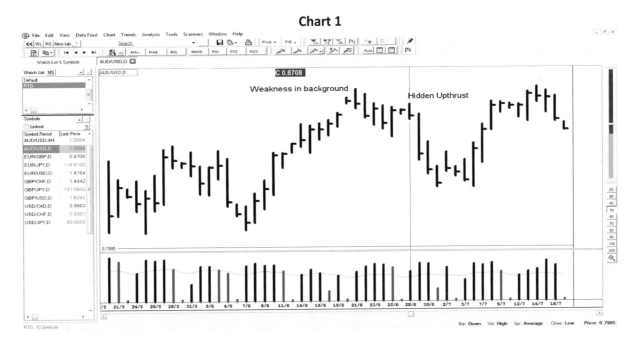

GH: What is your favorite VSA trade set-up to the short side?

SB: A *Hidden Up-thrust* after a *Buying Climax* has appeared in the background. I like to wait for a second lower high.

Chart 2

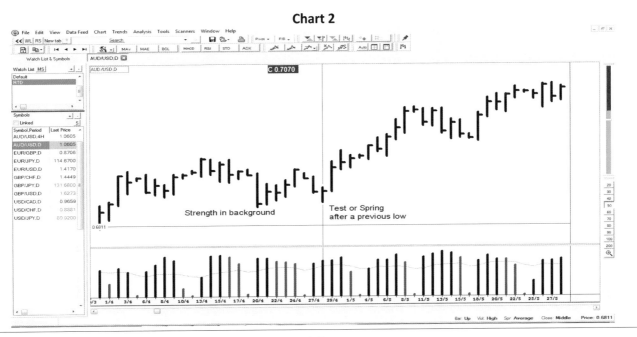

GH: Do you use any trading methods other than VSA?

SB: No. It took me a long time to master VSA. Why dump it and start on something else? If it works, why fix it?

GH: What advice would you give to a trader or investor who has just found VSA and wants to move to the next level of understanding?

SB: Work hard, study hard, never give up, ask lots of questions, and go to the seminars. You must ask questions if you're bewildered. Be clean, smart, and hungry. Find all the available information you can. There are many groups studying Wyckoff and the VSA Club is one of the best.

Making Volume Work for You
By Sebastian Manby

It is no secret that professional traders have one advantage over the private trader: they can read Volume, but not only that, they have been known to hide Volume from you for periods of time in order to have an advantage over you, large orders at certain levels above or below the market. These large banks and brokerage houses claim that in order to make a market, they need an edge over the rest of the crowd. Large orders that are processed do not appear on the tape as it would show up on the radar of other professional traders who would change their bid/offers or pull orders as large blocks go through the ticker tape showing strength or weakness appearing suddenly. The professional trader uses only the price and Volume and usually no other indicator to read the true balance of supply and demand as Wyckoff preached at the turn of the century.

The study of price and Volume and their relationship is vital to detect turning points in the market as professional operators have large amounts of capital and need to work this capital to make money. This cannot be done by buying at the market or limit orders as this would de-stable prices causing an unreadable situation, so whip sawing is used to shake out the crowd and catch stop losses, but the real reason is to process large orders while covering your strategy and not giving the game away at the same time. When the market starts to trend, then we say the large operators have control. These large operators know that there are not hundreds of stop losses, but thousands, and this gives them the opportunity to process large orders and conceal their true intentions as they attract other traders who can see their actions and act immediately to better their own accounts by reading Volume.

The other advantage professional traders will have is the news. They will already have the news in advance and will position themselves to take advantage and wrong foot as many traders as possible. Again by using the news to gun for stop losses and mislead the crowd into thinking the opposite of the operators true intentions. Why is it that bad news always appears in the last two weeks of a bear market and good news always appears at the top of a bull market?

It is done to put you under pressure at the bottom, and give you the feel good factor and hunger to load up with stocks etc. at the top of a bull market. This allows the operators to unload large blocks of stock or futures contracts at the best possible prices and to re accumulate at the bottom to increase profits to the operator at usually a large loss to the crowd. The cycle is then repeated over and over, giving us bull markets and bear markets, thus the reason why you are bombarded day and night with news, earning, unemployment, payrolls etc. These operators know that three things in the market, Fear, Hope, and Greed rule you. Fear of missing out, hope that when you are losing, that prices will recover and you can close out break even, and greed that when you have a profitable position, you hang on for greater profits and often fail to see the tide coming in.

By studying Volume and its relationship to price, you can begin to detect subtle changes in supply and demand, and you will see when the large operators are active, and by observing the results of their actions, you should begin to see the path of least resistance building a picture of the on-going market unfolding before you in the trading session. If you were to be sitting in front of your computer one day and see a large amount of Volume on an up bar, you would 'because you have been told' assume that strength always appears on up bars, and weakness always appears on down bars. Because you have read this in books and magazines, you would take this at face value and believe this to be true. In actual fact, up bars with excessive Volume is weakness, as down bars with high Volume shows strength. How can this be true?

Well imagine you are an operator with a large block to dispose of, how can you do this without putting the price against you? This would mean marking up the price to bring in buyers. Rising prices create demand; demand does not create rising prices. If you see prices rising, you are more likely to buy than sell, as you would expect to make a profit as prices continue to rise, but if you cannot read Volume; your image of these rising prices would distort the true picture as you would think it bullish, you would not see excessive Volume indicating weakness.

Reading one bar in the chart does not give you the complete picture, it is also the result of this high Volume that we would be very careful to observe, does the market top out? Do prices start to fall back?

This would indicate that supply had swamped demand, capping the top of the market but this might only be the start of distribution, one high Volume bar on its own does not create a bear market, but usually marks the start of supply. So by reading the Volume, we are able to detect that the large operators we active and that their opinions had changed and were probably turning bearish, but because you could not read Volume, you would think the market would keep rising and maybe buying on the reactions. The operators would know that the crowd were soaking up all they could and will artificially hold prices up until all has been unloaded, this would be characterized by a low Volume up bar (No demand). This would indicate to the large operators that the buying had dried up and the mark down can begin.

The opposite would be true when the operators have marked prices down far enough that they can cover at a large profit any short positions, usually a loss to the crowd who are now panicked in to selling out in fear of even lower prices, usually on bad news. Thus the cycle is repeated over and over. By reading the Volume with price, you can learn to trade successfully in any time frame, as you will begin to know the real movements from the false. There are a lot of false drives in the market, which are deliberately done to trick you into losing money. This is how the professional operators stay in business, but by understanding the different intensities that appearing the market, you can make money too, all you have to do is follow the operators, when they move, you move too.

So all I have to do is sit back and wait for the operator to tell me when? Well it's not that simple, because Volume is the powerhouse of the market, we have to observe the corresponding price action, is there an old trading area to the left?

If you see low Volume down bars with a narrow spread, then this would indicate that the professional operators were bullish and that they would be willing to absorb the supply as they reached the old top. However, if you see low Volume on up bars as the market approaches the old top, then this would indicate that the market was weak and it would be fairly safe to short near this old top, this would also be true for trend lines. Trend lines are the railroad for prices when the market is trending strongly, and we would be looking for support or resistance as these trend lines are approached.

For example: if you see a wide spread on increased Volume as it approaches an old trend line (or old top or bottom) we would expect this to be broken, but if we see no demand (weakness) or a test (strength) we know that it will not be broken and we can place our orders and make a profit as we can read the path of least resistance. Imagine the path of least resistance to be water running down a hill, it would not just run down in a straight line, it would twist and turn if obstacles were in the path, so the path of least resistance would be the easy path, not necessary the quickest one. This is how the operators mark prices round to find Volume, if there are large orders at a certain price, the operator might avoid that price level as it would mean he would have to absorb this supply at higher levels, and a quick way to go broke. This is why we have shakeouts and whipsawing in the early stages of a rally, because it not cost effective to absorb ever-increasing supply at higher levels.

Volume is the key to the truth.

-Sebastian Manby

CHAPTER 12
Advice from the Master, Tom Williams

G: I'm here with Tom Williams in Worthing, South of England and we're going to talk about Volume Spread Analysis. More importantly, what *is* Volume Spread Analysis? So Tom, perhaps for the people here, you can explain what Volume Spread Analysis is.

T: Gavin, thank you. Well for short, we call it VSA. Volume. Spread. Analysis. It's really self-explanatory. To analyze a chart you have to look at the Volume, and on that Volume you will want to notice what the price has done on that Volume, like has it moved up, down or has it gone sideways? Those ingredients will give you the answer to the market, in most cases. It is always there in hindsight, so if you look back at price action, all these principles that we talk about are there, but if you don't see them at the live edge of the market, you obviously need to put some more study in. So again, if they are there in hindsight, they must be near at the live edge of the market.

If you were to be sitting in front of your computer one day and see a large amount of Volume on an up bar, you would assume, because you have been told, that strength always appears on up bars, and weakness always appears on down bars. Since you have read this in many books and magazines, you would take this at face value and believe this to be true. In actual fact, up bars with excessive Volume is weakness, as down bars with high Volume shows strength. How can this be true?

Well imagine you are an operator with a large block of stocks or shares to dispose of, how can you do this without putting the price against you?

You would have to mark up the price to bring in buyers. Rising prices create demand, but demand does not create rising prices. If you see prices rising, you are more likely to buy than sell, as you would expect to make a profit as prices continue to rise. But, if you cannot read Volume, your image of these rising prices would distort the true picture as you would think it bullish and you would not see excessive Volume indicating weakness.

Now what people have to realize, is that this is not using any mathematical formulae at all. It's just purely looking at the supply and demand from the 'professional side' of the market. It's very reliable and it works, and we can prove it works because we have software that comes up with signals of what I call, 'uncanny accuracy'. They only appear automatically on a live feed without the intervention of human beings, if you get the logic right. Many traders out there have some good ideas, but when they test them, they're lucky they work 40% of the time. You will notice that the indicators generated by using VSA are approximately 90% accurate. You might think that 90% accuracy is wonderful, but you can't forget that there are two sides of making money in the market.

First, you need to be able to analyze the market, which you find is very tricky in a way. We'll explain why, but the other skill is you must be a good trader, a good trader in your own right. You need to be able to pull that information and put it to some good use to turn it into money.

Now Volume is the most important ingredient. Keep in mind that the average bank in the city of London will fill two telephone directories per day with their orders. That's just one bank, one merchant bank, so that's just to give you an idea of the Volume that's involved here. What you're looking at is a consensus of opinion from the professional side of the market. Not all these professionals communicate with each other. They all work in isolation. If they are making a bad trade, they will close out very quickly and switch their positions and that's for sure. So Volume is extremely important.

Now when you see the varying amounts of Volume, which may be high, it may be very high, or it may even be average, or it can be low - it all means something very, very important, but that only gives you half of the information. The other half of the information is in the price movements, or the price 'Spread'.

G: In other countries like America, they call it the 'range' of the bar.

T: The 'range' of the bar- yes, that's what it is called in America.

G: Yes, let's be clear, we've talked about the Volume, but the range or Spread of the bar is the 'high' or the 'low' of the price bar, in any time frame. It doesn't matter what it is, but it gets to a high point and it gets to a low point before it closes, but then eventually it closes. You can look at a 1 minute bar or a daily bar- all the principles are the same.

T: The close is very important. We don't even use the open. Openings are usually used by people who are using mathematical formulae. Mathematical formulae have been around for nearly 30 years. Now, I'm not going to belittle them, but if you are an expert in any of those fields, what you could do is use VSA, too. If VSA is backing up what your expertise formula is telling you, then you're probably right. If it's not backing it up, perhaps you will want to tread cautiously and trade only one or two contracts if you usually trade 10 or more. So it is definitely a super way of backing up any other systems.

You can even back up newspaper reports with it just to see when a newspaper is telling the truth or not. Of course newspapers use fundamentals and sometimes they're right, sometimes they're wrong.

G: Tom, may I ask you another question? Many traders I talk to are using technical analysis, which you said is based on mathematical formulae. There are many, many ways to analyze charts based on technical methods. I know there are thousands of books on it and many of the tools available will look back on the past price movement to analyze and try to predict the future price movement.

In fact, most of the retail traders I talk to use some form of technical analysis because that's what almost everybody uses to consider what they think is high probability trade set-ups. Often, from what I hear, the system will give them a green or red indicator based on the past price, and as they enter that position, the market moves heavily against them. It's almost always at the top, they will come in and buy at the top or they're going to sell at the bottom.

Now, can you explain to us why you developed Volume Spread Analysis and how is it so different from a standard technical analysis indicator?

T: Well, my story was that I went to the United States in my late 20's and went looking for a job. I was lucky enough to fall in with somebody who happened to be a part of a charter trading syndicate. These are groups of people who get together that have large sums of money at their disposal. Only sometimes would they trade other peoples' money.

These traders would accumulate or distribute the underlying stocks. It's very, very profitable. It's this accumulation and distribution of the underlying stocks that is actually causing the bull moves and the bear moves.

Now I was really good at technical drawing. I use to draw these huge charts, they would cover a desk, and I would model the high, low, close, and the Volume. Honestly, I really had no exact idea of what I was drawing for at least two years. Then one day, one of the syndicates suggested, actually, the owner suggested that I take the Wyckoff course and they also paid for it. It was $500 dollars in those days and it was located out in Park Ridge, right by Chicago. I studied the course for about a year until it all slowly started to fall into shape.

Don't forget there were no computers around, no futures- it was all stocks and shares, commodities, and options. That's how I got started and I did very, very well and retired at 40. I went back to England and this was the time computers were just becoming available to the public. I believe IBM just started promoting their first desktop because I recall this was when Bill Gates got involved.

Now I didn't know the first thing about computers. I'm still no good at it! But I wondered if the information and knowledge I had learned from the syndicate could be computerized. The reason why I thought that was because I was sure if a computer could do it, it would remove the emotional factor from trading. A computer has no emotions, it can't feel or see emotions, so the logic you put into the computer is either right or not right, and it is as simple as that. So then I employed a programmer to do this, which was and is very expensive, I might add!

Low and behold, I gave the info to the programmer, and luckily, he was able to reproduce what I was telling him to form into a series of signals. That's how VSA started.

G: To recap, this program is completely unique to TradeGuider and you had the good fortune of spending so many years with the syndicate learning how they traded. Now I remember you telling me a story of how the market, or markets, can be somewhat manipulated and you get misinformation. However, the 'Smart Money' cannot hide their intentions in Volume. So the misinformation is what causes the emotional decision making process for each individual trader, which causes them to lose money because in affect, what a market is doing is giving you information. You hear information about the market from many places like the TV, newspapers, friends, your broker, etc. There's so much information for the trader, it's almost impossible to decide.

But the two things that you told me that have stuck with me are that chart never lies if you know how to read it correctly, and many of the retail traders are losing money. Many of them can be successful if they do one thing, namely the opposite of what they're doing now.

That comes tongue-in-cheek, but can you elaborate on those two points? Why the charts never lie and why is the retail public consistently losing money? Since VSA is here to help them, please elaborate.

T: It's well known that 85% of all options never exercise. That means 85% of all options must be losing. It's also fairly well known in circles that 50% of all stock traders lose money. You only hear the good things, you don't hear about the 50% that lose money trading stocks and shares. Futures are horrendous, 90% or more of futures traders lose money, and of course, the markets do not want you there to make money, so they do everything conceivable to put you off.

G: Who is 'they', Tom, you mention 'they'? Who exactly are 'they'?

T: Who are 'they'? Well the professional money, or the 'Smart Money'. What they do if they see an opportunity is manipulate the market and take full advantage of anything that happens to distribute or accumulate the market they are trading.

G: I just want to be clear - your methodology works in all markets, whether it's stocks, foreign exchange, spot forex and the VSA the methodology, namely the TradeGuider software, works in ALL markets where there is available Volume, is that correct?

T: That's right. This is because it's traded by human beings, and you will find human beings will trade markets in certain ways. Different intensities, yes, but they all basically trade the same way. They have to accumulate a line, and then they have to mark it up and resell it. If you think about it, any business on the planet works that way. If you're a shopkeeper, you have to buy wholesale, you have to present it nicely, mark it up, and then you have to resell it. That's how you run a business. That's how you do it in the stock market. Huge amounts of money are in the stock market purely because they want to trade it and make profits from it.

G: Not just the stock market, it is all markets. Markets are made up of traders, individuals, banks, large institutions and syndicates. You were a member of one of those syndicates, which is why VSA was created. It's for the retail trader.

Now, I often get asked about the reason you blew the whistle as to what is really going on. What made you decide to give your knowledge to the general public? You were given very privileged information since you were invited into a syndicate. You didn't have to retire, but you could have made your own syndicate and made millions. What was your reasoning behind that?

T: The main reason was the advent of the computer. Without these computers, without the Internet, you really couldn't go far at all. Now with the advent of the computer and Internet, it made things far easier. Don't forget, I had to draw all the charts by hand. You could only realistically track 10-12 instruments like cattle, corn, or a stock. That was the reason- along with the fact I was only 40 when I retired and still very, very active. Naturally, I still thought the subject was so fascinating, so I decided to computerize it. Now the reason I wrote *"The Undeclared Secrets that Drive the Markets"*-

G: Now called *"Master the Markets"*-

T: Yes, *"Master the Markets"*. The reason I wrote that book was so that VSA software buyers could read the book in a day or so and have an extremely good idea of what it's all about. They would get a good idea of what they were looking at. The thing is, you can rely on it. It's very accurate. The Volume is showing you the amount of activity that's actually taking place amongst the professional money operators.

G: To end this particular session, many people will read this and some traders will be experienced yet still be losing money, some experienced traders will be gaining money, or some will be new and just beginning, like I was, 9 years ago when we first met. What would be your advice to anyone wanting to make money in the markets? What would you advise them to do?

T: First of all, I would emphasize how treacherous and dangerous the market really is. That's the first thing you need to understand. The market does not like you, it does not want you there, and you're there for one reason only- to be one of the losers. For the market to work, you need to have far more losers than winners. It's like a pyramid. It won't work if everybody is a winner. It can't work. That's what drives the stock market, the markets work to put you off.

The single reason for that is the professional money. The professional market has to sell into up bars, which immediately deters people and then to buy on down bars, which again, deters people. When the professional money buy on a down bar, the news is most likely guaranteed to be bad. So the would-be trader thinks, "Oh I can't buy on this, despite what that Tom Williams said... No, no, it is falling, the news is all bad, no, no, no..."

But that is professional money stepping into the market buying against the bad news and the same is true for the top. The news will always deter you from a perfect trade.

G: It's almost like people who read or hear this will have to re-evaluate their thinking. By natural instinct, if you see and hear good news and the market rises, you will want to buy. The same goes for if you see or hear bad news and the market falls, you want to sell. However, with VSA, it's the other way around, and actually, it's the truth.

So Tom, thank you. It will make sense to people who read this, but the secret is to look at the charts, then discern the reasons why. Look at where you lost money, look at where you got stopped out, and then evaluate why.

The great thing about charts is that they leave patterns and they tell you a story. If you can read those patterns, you can tell the story in the future. That means if you're live into the market, you will see these patterns and then you will understand by reading Tom's book and using the TradeGuider software that actually, when you think you should be buying, you should be selling and if you think about selling, you should be buying.

And that's the way the markets work. Thank you, Tom.

Photo by Jay L. Clendenin

The Solitary Trader
Tim Rayment

By Kira McCaffrey Brecht

In his own words, Tim Rayment, 49, describes his early years as "a childhood of just enough poverty to create ambition."

Indeed that ambition has taken Rayment far. Not only is he an accomplished and honored British journalist, but once he shifted his focus, energy and time to trading, he has chalked up substantial success and accolades in that arena as well.

Whopping 44 Percent Gain

Now a full-time currency trader, Rayment earned first place in the 2009 World Cup Trading Championships forex division.

In my one-hour phone interview with Rayment to his remote home in the United Kingdom countryside, I quickly learned that he is a person who does not

rest on his laurels. Indeed, he shrugged off my congratulatory comments. "I was very disappointed with my performance in 2009. It should have been better. The average true range is 120 pips at this moment. That means that the euro moves 0.9 percent per day," Rayment says.

Hard Driving

His hard-driving work ethic is no doubt in part behind his success in the trading world. Rayment finds participating in the World Cup contest as helpful because "it gives you nowhere to hide. You can't pretend to yourself you are trading well if you are not.

"One of the things I like best about trading is it will find any weakness. There is no room for complacency. If you get a little lazy, the market will punish that laziness in an instant. It is a perpetual challenge. You are learning all the time," he says.

Writing Led to Trading

He earned an English degree at the University of Leeds in the U.K. In 1982, Rayment started his career as a cub newspaper journalist at a small local paper in a tiny fishing village called Grimsby.

Rayment recalls the morning routine at the office in which all the reporters spent the first half hour perusing national papers looking for a potential local tie-in to research and write about. Each morning Rayment gravitated to the Financial Times and Lloyd's List, a shipping paper.

"I would pick up Lloyd's List because Grimsby is a fishing port. I thought, I'm going to get some fishing stories from a shipping paper. And I knew instinctively it was important to understand economics to some extent."

Rayment quickly moved up the journalism ladder, and at age 24, he became the youngest reporter on The [London] Sunday Times. "Newspapers suit me because I'm the solitary type—sociable but capable of long periods of isolation," Rayment says.

Truth and Reality

He found similarities between his two careers. "Trading is like journalism. It gives you a connection to the world at large," Rayment says. Also, while working as a reporter, he found that "many stories, as told by governments or banks—whether they are economic, political or business in nature—are not quite as they first appear. The challenge is to be alert and to search for the underlying reality or truth."

The same could be said for the markets.

Dabbling in the Markets

It was not until nearly a decade later that Rayment began dabbling in the financial markets. He started following U.K. warrant prices in the newspaper. "I liked the volatility, and I thought I could make some money trading," he remembers.

During the next several years, while continuing his full-time work at the Times, Rayment

tried trading bonds and index futures. "It wasn't based on anything really. All I can say is that I traded amateurishly."

However, Rayment tasted something that he liked: "It is probably the same for any retail trader who doesn't know what they are doing. You get a taste of something that is challenging and exciting," he says.

Early Mentor

In 1998, Rayment had the good fortune to connect with Tom Williams, the creator of Volume Spread Analysis. "I rang him, and he was very reluctant to sell me his software. He said, 'Trading is very difficult, you know.' I insisted and agreed that I would pay £5,000 in installments," Rayment says.

"These days if I'm asked by someone who is starting out in trading for advice, the first place I send them is the Trade Guider website. For me, it demystified the markets to a great extent," Rayment says.

Boulders in the Path

Rayment stumbled over his own personality traits in the early part of his trading career, but now finds this mindset helps him succeed.

WRITING ABOUT ROGUE TRADERS

Before earning accolades in the world of trading, Tim Rayment was the British Press Awards Feature Writer of the Year in 2001, which is the equivalent to a Pulitzer Prize in the U.S.

"Some of the Sunday Times work has been fast-moving and dangerous. Such a background is helpful for trading calmly under stress," Rayment says.

Read Rayment's story on Joseph Cassano, the multimillionaire trader accused of bringing down the insurance giant AIG and with it the world's economy in The Sunday Times.

TRADING & MURDER IN THE U.K. COUNTRYSIDE

Tim Rayment rented an isolated farm in the U.K. countryside for nine years. During that period, he completed intensive study of the Tom DeMark methodology, which he has incorporated into his current trading approach.

The farmhouse is quite well-known because a criminal plot to debase England's currency was carried out there in the 18th century," Rayment explains.

"I was studying DeMark in the former home of David Hartley, 'the King of the Coiners.' So, I was planning to take my clippings from the currency legally, in the same 12th-century farmhouse where he had planned to take his clippings illegally 200 years earlier," he says.

Rayment's predecessor in the building was executed for murdering the tax inspector sent from London to see what was going on. Read the story of the Yorkshire Coiners.

"I am an independent-minded person. In the early part of my trading career, that wasn't helpful because I didn't accept anything at face value. It wasn't until I proved that advice was sound by losing money [doing the opposite thing] that I would accept it," he says.

Now, "for a more experienced trader, an independent mind is a prerequisite. The best opportunities lie when you are the other way from the crowd," he explains.

Studying DeMark

The next step in his trading journey was to study the work of trader and analyst Tom DeMark. He now uses a methodology of his own creation that combines Volume Spread Analysis and DeMark's work and indicators.

"I did a lot of work on trading strategies when I lived on a farm that was very isolated. The only light you could see at night was the light on in my kitchen. It was a very good place for a trader to be," Rayment says.

"I work best when I work entirely alone," he continues.

Diving into Forex

In 2003 Rayment moved to the forex arena. "I chose currencies because, as the most liquid market on earth, the trading strategies can be scaled to any size," he says.

"Currencies are also difficult, which appeals to my need to be challenged—I don't like any endeavor to be easy," he adds.

Bottom line? Rayment says, "I think it's possible for a disciplined trader to achieve 35 percent a year without leverage from the currency markets."

His Method

In his trading, Rayment seeks to "identify moments where the crowded trade is wrong."

"I'm a genuine countertrend and reversal trader. I certainly don't try to pick tops and bottoms," he says.

He trades using a daily chart as an anchor and monitors 15 currency pairs for opportunities. His average holding time is one to three days.

Being Human

Trading, at its most unforgiving, forces one to face personal weaknesses. Rayment concludes that "you need a degree of introspection to balance your flaws as a human being."

Rayment has moved from the infamous farmhouse (see sidebar) to a converted mill. "I have two children. I am a parent. [But] I live and work alone," he says.

"The most important room is the one that has 10 screens in it," Rayment concludes. He is probably sitting there right now.

Isn't it time
YOU
join the
Smart Money?

I wish you good trading, constant profits, and belief that you can have anything you want if you take massive action now!

-Gavin Holmes
gavin@tradingintheshadow.com

For free educational resources visit my website
www.tradingintheshadow.com

Printed in Great Britain
by Amazon

64767253R00091